REDBOOK'S
Nannies,
Au Pairs, &
Babysitters

How to find and keep the right in-home child care for your family

REDBOOK'S

Nannies, Au Pairs, & Babysitters

How to find and keep the right in-home child care for your family

Jerri Wolfe, Ph.D.

Hearst Books
New York

Library of Congress Cataloging-in-Publication Data

Wolfe, Jerri. L.
  Nannies, Au Pairs & babysitters : how to find and keep the right in-home childcare for your family / [by Jerri Wolfe].
        p. cm.
  Includes bibliographical references and index.
  ISBN 1-58816-004-1
  1. Nannies—United States. 2. Au pairs—United States. 3. Babysitters—United States. I. Title: Nannies, Au Pairs, and babysitters. II. Title.

HQ778.63 .W65 2001
649—dc21
                                                                    00-040709

Printed in Hong Kong
First Edition
1 2 3 4 5 6 7 8 9 10

Illustrations by Sally O. Lee
Cover photo: © Photonica
Design and layout: Leslie Haimes
Produced by Packaged Goods

www.redbookmag.com

Contents

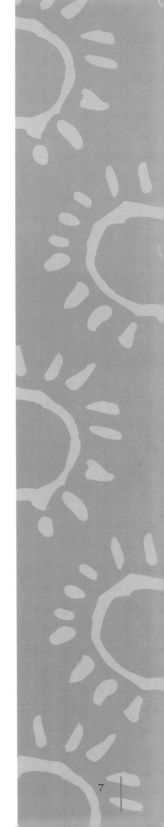

Introduction: Is In-Home Child Care Right for You?

"It's the same every weekday. Jon and I are up at 6 A.M. to face another day of traffic, phone calls, and meetings. Luckily Sam and Erin, ages two and three, don't have to face the early morning traffic with us. Each morning they get to sleep until they want, and then roam around the house in their PJs, and lately they've been building wonderful forts with Stephanie, their nanny. That's what I want for my kids—to be able to spend time in the comfort of their own home, with their own toys and our family's routines."

The Advantages

There are a variety of reasons why families choose in-home child care. Like Sam and Erin's parents, many families want their children to have the security that comes from spending days in familiar surroundings, as well as the opportunity to develop a relationship with one consistent caregiver. Other families' primary reason for choosing in-home care is the control over the quality of care that their children receive. For these families, the caregiver is seen as an extension of parental care as the parents partner with the caregiver to plan the daily schedule, activities and guidance. Enduring friendships frequently develop as parent and caregiver share the challenges and celebrate the children's milestones. An added advantage experienced by many families with in-home care is the opportunity for both children and parents to experience another culture, when the caregiver comes from another country. Obviously, for families with children who have special needs, finding a caregiver who can give their child specialized attention is a priority. In-home child care is often their best choice. In comparing in-home care to day care, families choosing the former site the reduced exposure to illness, ease of providing care for a sick child, and flexibility of scheduling that is provided by in-home care.

The Disadvantages

In-home child care does have its disadvantages, and parents should consider them carefully before choosing this style of care. Selecting the right care provider is crucial— for unless you are working in your home with your caregiver, she is working unsupervised. It is important to understand when considering an in-home care provider that a significant amount of your time will be required in the beginning to cultivate a relationship. If you do not have the time or are not interested in developing this type of relationship, then in-home care is not for you. In addition, families should consider their need for privacy. An in-home caregiver will be privy to your home when it's at its messiest; to your children when they are their worst behaved; and to you on those (rare) occasions when you are hurried, overwhelmed, and grumpy. Another drawback is a potential illness or emergency by the caregiver, leaving you suddenly without childcare. Families who choose in-home care avoid this problem by developing a back-up plan for such emergencies. Before choosing in-home care, families need to carefully examine the financial requirements of the options they are considering. The cost of in-home care varies greatly depending on the type of care you need; however it can be the most expensive care available. And remember, if you hire an in-home caregiver, you are the employer and are required to follow the laws regarding domestic workers.

Is In-Home Child Care Right for You?

Advantages

Security of familiar surroundings.
Consistency and bond with one caregiver.
Parents control quality of care.
One-on-one focus for the needs of the child.
Flexible scheduling.
Care available if child is sick.

Disadvantages

Locating/assessing proper candidates not always easy.
Time commitment in getting to know and working in
    partnership with caregiver.
Caregiver's work is largely unsupervised.
Some loss of privacy.
Unexpected break in care due to caregiver illness or emergency.
Research and compliance with domestic employment laws.

Four different families, four different types of child care

Nanny Live-In

"I didn't know if we were ever going to find the right nanny. We had exhausted nearly all our options when finally we found Gabriela. She came to us six years ago when we had two children, a one year old and a ten year old. We knew she was the right person for our family when we saw how lovingly she interacted with our baby. She was highly recommended from her previous employer. Two years ago we added another baby to our family and Gabriela's help with both the new baby and the other children helped me stay sane during this period of late nights, bottles, and messy diapers. After all we have gone through together, Gabriela and I communicate very well—she often anticipates our needs and takes care of things before I even mention them. Gabriela is like one of our family, we really care for her, we celebrate her birthday, include her in our holiday activities, and try to show our appreciation—often and in many different ways—for the important role she plays in our family. We have a very full life. I don't know how we would make it without someone like Gabriela."

Nanny Live-Out

"We have had two wonderful nannies. Both women were in their 60s, each had raised six children of their own and so they knew how to raise kids. We hired Marianne when our first son Patrick was born. Two and a half years later our second son, Simon, was born. Marianne was always there for the children. Her judgment about what was in the children's best interests was excellent and I never had to worry about her being inappropriate. I learned a lot from Marianne. It was difficult for me to say goodbye after five years when our family moved out of state. Our second nanny, Anne, was also a great caregiver. She was very reliable and responsible with our sons. Her style was different from Marianne's, and I had to adjust to her less-assertive, more reserved temperament. But like Marianne, she spent a lot of time interacting with the boys, playing board games, and doing craft projects. She read to them, and drew with them each day. A distinct advantage that an older nanny brought to our family was stability and continuity. The boys and I found great comfort in the gentle rhythm of their days with Anne and Marianne."

Au Pair

"After our live-out caregiver left us, we decided to look into the possibility of having someone live in. We felt this would be more dependable and flexible. At the time we had two boys, a three-year-old and a seven-year-old. Our first au pair, Caroline, was from Sweden. Caroline's responsibilities included getting our older son up, dressed, and out to the school bus on time. She also prepared his lunch and made breakfast for both boys. Most of her day was spent caring for our toddler. She would not only ensure his safety while we were at work but also provided him with a very interesting day. She would play with the boys outside and even have picnics in the winter! She would teach them Swedish games and bake with them when the weather did not allow for much else. She would even dress up the breakfast table with a flower and share her culture as often as possible. We were so impressed with the interaction she had with our children, we have continued to use au pairs. Each year that we say goodbye to one au pair we also look forward to getting to know a new one."

Babysitter

"When Thomas was born, I worked out of a home office and had occasional, irregular meetings. By cutting back my hours and working on weekends I could get most of my office work done, but I still needed child care for three to four hours, five times a month. Due to my irregular child care needs I went in search of a person who was available during the days, didn't need regular employment, and was interested in caring for a baby. The first thing my husband and I did in our search was to brainstorm a list of people we could tell of our need. We had found word of mouth to be useful in other situations and it didn't let us down this time. Michele (a friend of a friend) began caring for Thomas when he was three months old. Michele worked in retail and, because she was in charge of scheduling, could arrange to get those specific days off. For Thomas, having Michele come over was a treat. At three years old, Thomas had been in the care of Michele for as long as he could remember. Michele has rocked him to sleep many times and navigated him through ear infections or just general grumpiness. Michele always gets down on her knees and gives Thomas a big hug and an enthusiastic "Hello." She has really been a blessing to me."

Creating Your Own Success Story

Will you be lucky and find a situation like the ones previously described?

While luck does play a part, a carefully planned hiring process will help you find the right caregiver, and thoughtful, on-going dialogue with your caregiver will be necessary to create seamless day-to-day care for your children. While the specifics of every family's child care situation are unique, a few important factors apply to all child care situations. A successful situation requires finding an individual to whom you can entrust the well-being of your children and your home. You'll want a person who is reliable, willing to respect your rules, able to communicate concerns, and willing to seek solutions with you to the issues that will no doubt come up. As the employer, you need to provide competitive pay, support your child(ren)'s relationship with the caregiver, and be respectful of her experience, opinions, and needs. When evaluating the caregiver's actions and decisions, take time to view her behaviors from her perspective. Background, culture, and experience influence the choices she will make. The skilled caregiver who feels trusted and valued is the one most likely to provide a warm, nurturing environment for your children.

From the child's viewpoint, a successful child-care situation is one in which the caregiver really, truly cares for him and gets to know all that is super neat about him. He wants a person who smiles a lot, has the patience to comfort him when he's sick, is willing to read the same story over and over, who says "no" when it's really important, and who will help him be successful as he works on the huge, and sometimes overwhelming, task of growing up.

CHAPTER 1

Defining Your Needs

Nanny, Au Pair, and Babysitter: which child care provider is right for you?

Nannies care for children in the home of their employers. A nanny may live in the home or may have other living arrangements and commute to her employer's home on a daily basis. Nannies are in charge of all tasks related to the care of children, including preparing and cleaning up after children's meals, laundry, and room tidying. Based on the parents' requirements, a nanny will plan the children's day to include personal care, meals, activities, play dates, and outings. Nannies come with more or less experience, depending on your needs: from credentialed "career nannies" to nannies with little formal training.

Au Pairs are individuals between the ages of 18–26 who come to the United States as part of an educational and cultural exchange program. The au pair program is operated under the auspices of the United States Department of State. While a nanny is an employee, the au pair is considered part of the family. In exchange for providing up to 45 hours a week of child care, au pairs receive a private room, a predetermined stipend, and often, medical insurance and monies to attend school. One year is the maximum stay in the United States allowed au pairs. Au pairs are placed and supported during their visit by authorized agencies. Generally, au pairs do not have any formal child-care education. It is best not to place au pairs in families with a child less than two years of age unless the au pair has at least two hundred hours of documented infant child-care experience.

Babysitters provide in-home care for families who do not need full-time child care. Babysitters are generally hired on a time-to-time basis and paid an hourly rate. Most babysitters lack formal child-care training and don't consider child care their profession.

Sharing Care

Do you want the benefits of having a nanny but feel concerned about the price? Many cost-conscious families share a nanny, dividing her day between households. This works particularly well for parents who work part time or have children in preschool for half the day. Another option is having the nanny care for both families' children together, with each home serving as the host in turns. Finding the right family to share care with is as important as finding the right caregiver. Be sure the family you are considering is flexible, easy to talk with, and willing to seek solutions to the challenges of a shared-care arrangement. To find a partner for sharing care, try putting a notice up at your workplace, public library, or place of worship; tell everyone you know (the grapevine can be very helpful), and consider taking out an ad in your local newspaper.

Several factors need to be considered in choosing the right type of child care for you.

Do you:	Nanny live-in	Nanny live-out	Au Pair	Babysitter
need regular full-time child care?	✗	✗	✗	
need regular part-time child care?		✗	✗	✗
need part-time child care at irregular times?			✗	✗
need child care more than forty-five hours a week?	✗	✗		
want a caregiver who lives in your home?	✗		✗	
want to host a young person as part of a cultural exchange?			✗	
want a caregiver with formal child care training?	✗	✗		
want a caregiver who can travel with your family?	✗	✗	✗	

Which of the three types of care most closely matches your needs? A family who values its privacy should consider a live-out nanny. Families interested in a live-in care provider have two options: a live-in nanny or an au pair. If you live in an area with a shortage of nannies, you may find working with the au pair program easier than locating a quality nanny. If you are looking for a person to come in three days a week for five hours a day, a babysitter is likely the best match for you.

Another important factor in your decision making is the cost of care: a live-out nanny is the most expensive, followed by the live-in nanny, the au pair, and the babysitter. To determine the cost in your local area, call local placement agencies and talk with friends who have experience with in-home care.

Writing Your Job Description

Having identified the type of child care that best meets your needs, the next step is to determine the specifics of the position. A well-written job description will help you stay focused during the job search, will help as you develop interview questions for screening candidates, and can be used during the trial period to evaluate your caregiver's performance on the job. In addition, a well-written job description helps prospective candidates determine how the position matches their own skills and requirements. Begin by considering these four elements: a general description of the job, duties and responsibilities, requirements, and compensation.

1. General Description

This is the first thing a potential caregiver will read. It should include the number of children, and their ages, the number of hours and how they are structured, whether the position is live-in or live-out and the commitment period.

Make a list of the tasks you want your caregiver to perform. Be as specific as possible. While most caregivers are open to the addition of tasks related to children, they rarely appreciate finding out after accepting a position that household tasks such as cleaning toilets or walking the dog are part of their job. Oftentimes, extra tasks added once a nanny has been hired translate to a short-term employee. Keep in mind the way you want your employer to treat you, and use that as a guideline. Three categories of tasks to consider are childcare responsibilities, child-related housekeeping duties, and other household duties. For example:

Child Care Responsibilities

Personal Care: Diapering, dressing, bathing, and grooming.

Meals: Preparing nutritious meals and snacks. Teaching appropriate manners.

Activities: Cuddle, rock, and sing to baby. Build forts and play hide-and-seek with our four-year-old. Planning outings to our favorite places and arranging play dates with friends. Monitor progress and completion of homework.

Transportation:
Provide safe transportation to and from scheduled activities and appointments.

Supervision: Ensure appropriate supervision at all times.

Guidance: Enforce family rules and consequences. Implement guidance strategies as discussed with parent.

Child-Related Household Activities

Laundry: Wash and put away all the children's laundry.

Maintenance of Children's Areas:
Daily pick up of children's bathing and play areas. Weekly cleaning of children's bathroom and bedrooms. Supervise child's cleaning of bathroom and bedroom.

Kitchen: Clean up after preparation of children's meal. Empty dishwasher as necessary.

Automobile: Weekly cleaning and vacuum of family car provided for nanny's use.

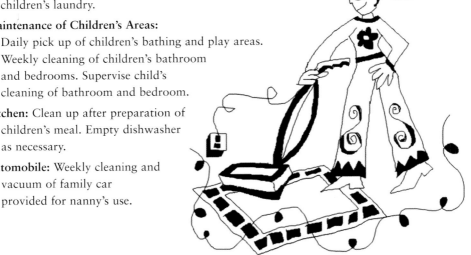

Other Household Activities

Housecleaning: Weekly cleaning of caregiver's room and bathroom. Weekly vacuuming of family living areas.

Meals: Clean kitchen following family breakfast.

Shopping and Errands: Run errands and pick up groceries as requested.

Pets: Supervise the cleaning of the hamster cage weekly.

Once you've made your list, look back over it and ask yourself "Can one person realistically complete all these tasks well?" Are most of your tasks child focused? If your list is heavy on cooking and cleaning, consider hiring a housekeeper or weekly service, thereby allowing the child-care provider to focus on her main task, the care of your children.

A bilingual caregiver can offer both the children and parents a wonderful opportunity to absorb a new language. However, it is essential that your caregiver speaks, reads, and writes in English well enough to:

- *Record the details of your child's day.*

- *Share daily high and lows.*

- *Fully understand the labels on medications and household products.*

- *Summon and instruct help in an emergency.*

- *Discuss guidance strategies.*

- *Express any concerns about the job arrangements.*

3. Requirements

After you have made the list of job expectations, consider the skills and traits needed for each task. If, for example, your caregiver will be transporting children, a driver's license and clean driving record should be required. Which of the following are important to your job?

Associate of Arts degree
Formal child-development training
Previous infant care experience
Previous child care experience
Special needs experience
CPR certificate
First aid certificate
Own car in working order
Driver's license
Clean driving record
Proof of auto insurance
Fluent in English
Nonsmoking
Valid work permit, if noncitizen

4. Compensation

A full-time nanny, live-in or live-out, will expect a weekly salary. The most sought-after candidates will likely be weighing other benefits as well. Time off, flexibility, and a myriad of other benefits can be a pivotal factor in the caregiver's decision-making process. The more generous your employment package, the longer a nanny is likely to stay. As an employer you will also be responsible for paying Social Security; Medicare; and federal, state, and city unemployment taxes on your caregiver's wages. Failure to comply with your tax obligations could result in criminal prosecution for perjury and tax evasion. You may also need to add worker's compensation insurance, which is inexpensive, to your home insurance policy. Additionally, some states require that you have unemployment insurance coverage: Your accountant will know if this applies to you. For au pairs, the salary and benefits are predetermined and include a stipend, medical insurance, and educational expenses. Babysitters are paid by the hour and typically do not receive additional benefits. Work by the hour usually runs one to two dollars higher than the salaried rate.

Salary

To set a fair wage, first determine the range of salary offered in your community. Several factors should be considered when determining where your job falls in that range. These include: live-in or live-out, the number of children cared for, special skills required for the job, number of hours required, responsibilities other than child-care, and benefits available. Salaries for live-out nannies are $100–150 per week more than for live-in nannies whose employers pay for room and board. Clearly, caregivers asked to work long hours, to manage three or more children, or to tend a special needs child will expect higher wages than those caring for one or two children 8:00 A.M. to 5:00 P.M. weekdays. Consider stating a salary range in the job description. Thus, you might pay a highly qualified candidate top dollar, or offer a less-qualified candidate the opportunity for a six-month raise if her work meets your expectations.

Wage Ranges for Live-In Nannies

$275/week for a young (18–20-year-old), inexperienced caregiver.

$300–$350/week for college graduates.

$350–$500/week for college graduates with previous experiences and most career nannies.

$500–$800/week in wealthy families for nannies with considerable experience, education, and savvy.

To determine the fair market rate for your area, consult the classified ads, check with friends, and contact placement agencies.

Many employers offer bonuses at six months or at a year for exceptional service. Nonperformance-based bonuses are frequently given at holiday time.

Days off

- Two or three weeks of paid vacation that can be taken in several ways: one week to coinciding with the family's vacation; one day per month (i.e., the third Tuesday of every month)—an arrangement whose predictability can be a boon; or a set number of vacation days to use at the caregiver's discretion, provided sufficient notice is given. You may want to require a certain period of employment before paid vacation can be taken.

- Paid holidays most frequently include New Year's Day, Memorial Day, Fourth of July, Labor Day, Thanksgiving Day, and Christmas Day. To avoid any misunderstandings due to culture differences, ask a caregiver you are seriously considering hiring about days off she needs due to traditional celebrations.

- Personal days cover illness, medical appointments, a death in the family, and other issues that require the caregiver to miss a day of work. Define how many days of paid personal leave are available and how those days accrue.

Transportation Benefits

If your caregiver will be using your car to transport children to and from activities, consider allowing the use of the car during off-hours. Caregivers who provide transportation for your children in their own vehicle should be given a monthly transportation allowance or reimbursement for mileage.

Insurance

An attractive benefit is medical insurance. Some families find that they can insure their caregiver on their own insurance. Other families provide a stipend to cover the cost or split the cost of group insurance the caregiver carries through a professional caregiver's association.

Checklist: Considering a Live-In?

Can you provide the minimum
   requirements?

- Private, furnished room
- Shared bathroom
- Meals

Which of these attractive features
   do you have to offer?

- Private bathroom
- Private entrance
- Telephone, private line,
  answering machine
- Small refrigerator
- Use of a car

Job Description: Live-Out Nanny

Provide loving care for two energetic children (ages 18 months and four years), Monday through Friday 7:00 A.M. to 6:00 P.M. A one-year commitment is required.

DUTIES AND RESPONSIBILITIES

Child Care Activities

Attend to day-to-day needs of the children including:

☐ Preparing a healthy breakfast, lunch, and snacks. Preparing the snack for our son's preschool class on our snack day (once a month).

☐ Diaper baby, and assist with dressing and grooming each morning.

☐ Plan activities including singing, dancing, reading, arts and crafts, fort building, and outdoor adventures.

☐ Drive four-year-old to and from afternoon preschool class.

☐ Offer guidance using positive parenting strategies as described by parents.

☐ Ensure child's safety at all times.

Child-Related Household Activities

☐ Develop a weekly menu for parents' approval. Add needed foods to the grocery list.

☐ Place all dirty dishes from meal preparation in the dishwasher. Empty dishwasher if needed. Wipe counters and sink. Store leftovers appropriately.

☐ Pick up children's bathroom daily. Clean bathroom weekly.

☐ Pick up family room and children's rooms daily.

☐ Launder and put away children's clothing.

Other Household Activities

☐   Assist the children in feeding and playing ball with the dog.

REQUIREMENTS

☐   Demonstrated skill in caring for young children—including creative activities and supervision. Formal training in child development preferred but not required.

☐   Good communication and problem-solving skills. Fluency in English.

☐   Own car in working order with proof of auto insurance. Valid driver's license and clean driving record.

☐   Current first aid certificate.

☐   Nonsmoking

☐   Three references

COMPENSATION

☐   Salary commensurate with experience.

☐   Monthly car allowance

☐   Two weeks of paid vacation after a year's service.

☐   Six paid holidays

☐   One day of paid personal leave for each month employed, can accrue up to two weeks per year.

☐   Bonus equal to two weeks' pay, upon satisfactory completion of the first year.

CHAPTER 2

Finding and Hiring a Good Care Provider

Two types of agencies help families locate in-home child care providers: agencies approved by the United States Department of State to conduct au pair programs and nanny placement agencies. Strict regulations govern au pair agencies and the services they offer. Licensed au pair agencies screen au pairs and families and provide matching services as follows:

- **Au Pair Screening:** All au pairs must have completed high school or the equivalent. In addition, the organization reviews references, provides a criminal background check, a medical evaluation, and a psychological profile test.

- **Family Screening:** Families are screened to determine their understanding of the au pair program and their suitability to serve as a host family.

- **Prematching:** Families are matched with an au pair based on child care needs, family interests, and lifestyle.

- **Travel Arrangements:** The agency coordinates all travel arrangements for the au pair's arrival and departure.

- **Orientation:** Sessions offer twenty-four hours of child-development instruction and eight hours of child safety training.

- **Support:** Ongoing support for the au pair/host family relationship through local care coordinators.

Nanny placement agencies, on the other hand, are not regulated in many states and vary greatly. The types of services offered by these agencies include:

- Recruiting and prescreening of child care providers.

- Providing families with candidates to interview who match their basic requirements.

- Assisting in the development of written employment agreements.

- Supporting caregivers by providing nanny networks.

- Helping providers and families access group insurance for the care provider.

Questions for Screening a Nanny Placement Agency

1. What types of caregivers do you place?

2. How do you go about matching caregivers to families?

3. Exactly how do you screen caregivers?

4. Do families have access to the file of a candidate whom they are considering hiring?

5. What is the cost of your service? How is the fee to be paid?

6. What if the caregiver doesn't work out?

7. How long have you been in business?

8. Will you send me some print material that describes your services and policies?

9. Will you provide the names and phone numbers of three families who have used your service?

Verifying the Right to Work

The Immigration Reform and Control Act of 1986 states that it is unlawful to knowingly hiring an alien who cannot legally work in the United States. When you hire a caregiver, you are required to verify she is a United States citizen, an alien with permanent residence, or holds a valid work permit. Call the Immigration and Naturalization Service at 1-800-870-3676 to request Form I-9, which details the procedures and documentation required. The first-time civil fine for knowingly hire an illegal alien ranges from $250 to $2,000.

Nanny placement agencies often have an application fee and a placement fee. Carefully check the policies regarding the placement fee of any agency you are considering. Placement fees are paid when you hire a caregiver sent to you by the agency and are either a fixed amount or a percentage of the salary. You will want to know what the agency's policy is if the caregiver doesn't work out. Some agencies state they will help you find a different caregiver if the first caregiver leaves within a certain period of time. If you find yourself in this situation, the agency will send you other caregivers to interview. However, you may feel pressured to select a less-than-ideal caregiver rather than lose the placement fee.

Before enlisting an agency to help you in your search, ask yourself "Does this agency provide a valuable service to my search? Is the agency representative pleasant and forthcoming with information?" While a good agency can save you time by providing a qualified pool of candidates and support you through your decision making, only you can choose the right caregiver for your family. One thing to remember is that you don't want to pass the decision making to someone else.

Our Story

"At age 60, Marianne was very different from anyone I thought I would hire. The image I had was of a young, energetic person. What was so impressive about Marianne was that during her twenty years as a nanny she had been with only five different employers. She showed me pictures of all the children she had cared for and told me about each one of them. I learned from this experience how important it is to keep an open mind when hiring."

Several options exist for locating a caregiver without the use of an agency. Begin by asking people in your community with in-home care providers their favorite recruiting strategies. The best places to advertise will vary from community to community. Places where potential employees are likely to look include:

- **Newspapers:** The local newspaper is a quick and effective way to get the word out in many communities. For best coverage, run your ad over a weekend. Don't forget to look in the "situations wanted" section, you might find a caregiver without having to place an ad yourself. If your area has a monthly family magazine, consider checking the classified ad section to see if there is a child-care section.

- **Community Bulletin Boards:** Many churches, preschools, clubs, and community centers provide space for flyers. Bulletin boards can also be found at grocery stores, medical centers, and other businesses serving children and families.

- **Local Colleges and Technical Schools:** Inquire at the school's job-placement office about procedures for posting a job opening. If the college has a child development or early childhood education department, ask if they have a newsletter or job board where you can place your advertisement.

- **Senior Centers:** Try checking your local yellow pages for agencies and organizations that cater to seniors.

- **Internet:** Enter the word "nanny" into your Internet search engine and you will find several Web sites focusing on nannies, some of which allow you to post a job notice.

Do not overlook the power of word of mouth. Let people know you are looking for a caregiver. You never know when someone will be letting go of a wonderful nanny because they no longer need her, or a friend may know of a wonderful college-age neighbor who would be great at providing after-school care.

Our Story

"I placed an ad in the newspaper for a nanny and received eighty responses. Based solely on the telephone screenings, I narrowed the field from eighty to two."

Nanny Wanted: Greenlake Area

Parents of lovable twin four-year-old boys looking for energetic nanny who loves to play with trucks, kick ball, and have fun. Live-out, full-time, must have own transportation, excellent driving record, and references. Terrific benefits. Call (555) 999-3333 and leave a message on the machine.

Advertisements

Whether you are placing an ad in a newspaper, on a bulletin board, or on the Internet, it should include certain basic pieces of information about the job: work hours, number and ages of children, duties, location, and contact number. Be sure to include other requirements that are unique to your situation. A carefully worded ad will screen out unqualified applicants and reduce your time on the telephone. If, for example, you are the parent of twin infants, your ad might state "experience and patience with infants required." An ad where space is limited, such as a classified ad, might look like this:

Caregiver needed for one five-year-old girl. Afternoons, 25 hours per week. Must have own car. Call Anna at (555) 222-4444 between 6:00–8:00 P.M.

If space allows, you might try to spice up an ad with information about your family, your location, or the position. Lead with your best selling points. You want potential caregivers to select your ad over the others with which it may be competing. Here are examples of enticing selling points:

To create an eye-catching bulletin board notice, you could use brightly colored or interestingly cut paper or attach one of your child's drawings. Bulletin board notices that include tear-off phone numbers make it easier for prospective applicants to respond to your ad.

> *Live-In Nanny* needed for two preschool-aged boys. Flexible schedule, not more than 40 hours, car provided. Treasure Valley. Call Mary at (555) 222-4444 between 6:00–8:00 P.M.

- Warm cozy cottage awaits the nanny who will care for our daughter.

- Parents who travel frequently seeking nanny to accompany children.

- Horse lover wanted to share weekday afternoons in the pasture with Lucky (the horse) and ten-year-old boy.

- Parents of two imaginative preschool girls looking for creative babysitter who loves to play pretend.

- Christmas in Hawaii with three-month-old Sara and her family.

Once the ad is placed you need to prepare to screen candidates over the phone. By taking the time now, you can assure yourself that only qualified applicants are invited for a personal interview. Your first goal for the phone interview is to determine whether the prospective candidate meets your basic requirements.

You might say:

"Sara, thanks for answering our ad for a nanny in yesterday's paper. We're looking for someone to care for our three-month-old daughter and our four-year-old son, Monday through Thursday, 7:00 a.m. until 4:00 p.m. and Friday, from 7:00 a.m. until noon. You must have your own transportation, as our son is involved in morning preschool and has to be taken and picked up daily. This is a live-out position. Does it sound appealing?"

If she seems promising, say:

"I'd like to ask you some additional questions. Is now a good time, or would you like to set a time to talk later in the day?"

Try to keep the list of questions and a pencil near the phone; that way, you are always ready to find out as much as you can about her qualifications and current situation. Be sure to jot down responses; after two or three interviews, memories are less than reliable.

If after a few questions you can tell she is not a good match for your job you could say:

"Thank you for your inquiry. It doesn't appear we are a good match for each other; we're looking for a person with significant experience with infants. Thank you for your time. I wish you the best of luck in your job search."

You may speak with a person who sounds like she has possibilities but you're not ready to schedule an interview until you've spoken to other candidates. In this case say:

"Right now we are calling everyone who responded to our ad. We hope to have this completed in the next week, and we'll start to schedule interviews shortly after."

When you find a strong candidate, say:

"You sound like you have the skills we are looking for. I'd like to send you a job description and a job application. Please review the job description and call if you have any questions. I look forward to receiving your job application in the mail and to talking to you further about our position. If you would give me your full name and address, I'll get that information out to you in the mail tomorrow."

Telephone Interview Questions

Experiences with Children
What experiences have you had working with children?
What ages of children have you worked with?
Do you have any formal childcare training?

Previous Job Experience
Tell me about your most recent job?
Why did you leave that position?
What other jobs have you held?

Personal
Do you smoke?
Where do you live? (Issue: commute time)
What makes you a good nanny?
What requirements do you have for employment?
  (i.e., pay, vacation, etc.)
When are you able to start?

Au Pair Interview Questions

The sponsoring agency will match you with an au pair and provide you with the au pair application packet. In many cases, they will also set up a phone interview for you. In addition to your other interview questions, here are a few you may wish to add to the list when you interview an au pair.

Why do you want to be an au pair?

What do you like most about caring for children?

What types of activities do you like to do with children?

How do you spend your free time?

Have you ever been away from your family for an extended period of time?

What will you do if you feel homesick?

Sample Job Application

Name _____ Phone _____

Address _____

City _____ State _____ Zip _____

Maiden name or other name used _____

Date of birth ___/___/___ Age _____ Social Security number _____

How long at current address? _____ If less than 2 years, list previous

Address _____

City _____ State _____ Zip _____

EMERGENCY CONTACT

Name _____

Address _____

Phone _____ Relationship _____

EDUCATION

Name of high school _____

Date of attendance _____

Year of graduation _____

Other schooling _____

Are you an American citizen?   ☐ yes   ☐ no

If not, do you have a green card or visa to work in this country?   ☐ yes   ☐ no

Do you have a current CPR certificate? _____

Do you have a current first-aid certificate? _____

Do you smoke?   ☐ yes   ☐ no

Are you allergic to pets?   ☐ yes   ☐ no

Do you have any health problems that would interfere with your ability to care

for children? _____

Have you ever been arrested or convicted of a crime?   ☐ yes   ☐ no

What are your reasons for becoming a nanny (au pair, babysitter)?

_____

_____

_____

_____

What are your long-term career goals? _____
_____
_____
_____

Are you interested in making a commitment to a position
as a nanny (au pair, babysitter) for at least one year? ☐ yes ☐ no

LIST THREE REFERENCES:

Name	Address	Phone	Relationship

EMPLOYMENT HISTORY (start with the most recent)

From—To	Position	Employer	Reason for Leaving

Do you have your own transportation? ☐ yes ☐ no
Driver's license number _____ License plate number _____
Make/Model of car _____ Insurance Co. and policy number _____
Do you have any tickets or accidents on your driving record? _____
Has your license ever been revoked? _____

PLEASE ATTACH THE FOLLOWING: Copy of your Social Security card
                               Copy of your driver's license
                               Proof of auto insurance
                               Copy of CPR certificate/first aid certificate
                               Copy of diplomas

I attest that all the above information is true and undestand that providing any
false information will disqualify me as a candidate

SIGNATURE _____ DATE _____

Plan on meeting your strong candidates twice. The first interview might take place away from your home and any other distractions (including children). Your goal is to learn as much basic information as possible. Second interviews are held in your home, in its natural state; child(ren), toys, and pets. To avoid potential conflicts, both parents—if living in the home—should participant in the hiring process. The person you select needs to be a good match with parents as well as children.

To set up the interview you might say:

"Hi, Maria, this is Sue Johnson. I was impressed with your job application and would like to meet with you to discuss the job further. Are you still interested? [If yes] Would Tuesday at 3:30 be a good time for you?"

The First Interview

Prior to the interview you need to sit down with your job description, the candidate's application, and a pad of paper. While you probably want to avoid reading questions directly from a sheet of paper, you will increase your comfort level and the effectiveness of the time with the candidate by thinking through the flow and content of the interview.

You can set the tone of the interview in the first few minutes. Start with a friendly introduction: "Hi, I'm Sue Johnson, it's so nice to meet you in person."

Next, try to describe what you want to accomplish in your time together.

"What I'd like to do today is to ask you some questions about yourself in an attempt to see if you are a good match for our family and this job. Please, feel free to ask me questions, too. I want you to be able to determine if the position fits your needs and interests."

Your first questions will be generated from the job application. Remember to ask questions that clarify or expand on the information in the application. Try to make questions opened ended (i.e., require more than a yes or a no answer). For example:

I see you are new to the area, what brought you here?

Tell me about what is involved in getting a _____ certificate?

What types of classes did you take in your early childhood program?

Did any classes involve direct experience with children?

What was your favorite class?

I see you worked for two years as a nanny for the Hawkins family. What were your responsibilities? Tell me about the child(ren)?

What were your biggest challenges in that position? Why did you leave that position?

What have been the high points in your experiences working with children?

What age child do you like working with the most?

Have you ever had to handle an emergency situation? Please describe what happened.

Next, ask questions that explore the candidate's position on the important points in your job description.

What are your career goals? What type of work would you like to be doing two years from now?

What are your favorite activities to do with children? How well do you swim?

Do you mind doing light household chores, like grocery shopping?

Do you have any commitments that would make it difficult for you to stay a bit late on an evening when one of us got held up in traffic?

Do you have any driving violations?

"What-if" questions will give you a glimpse into the candidate's style and experience with children. Be sure and develop questions that reflect real life in your house. Here are a few examples to help you get started.

What would you do if:

- Our two month old woke up from his nap crying very hard?

- When you announce that it is time to leave the park, two-year-old Eric says "no" and runs away from you?

- The rule is we stay in our yard and cross the street only with the grown up in charge. Three-year-old Madison walks into the street when she sees her friend Hillary come out of her house into the yard?

- Michael, our five-year-old, has built a racetrack with the blocks. Peter, age two, grabs one of the blocks from the track. Michael is yelling "no," and both boys are holding onto the block?

- The rule is homework is to be completed after school and before the television can be turned on. Jessica comes home from school, announces she's had a tough day and turns the TV on?

- While Sarah is napping, Isaac falls from his bike and gets a gash in his leg?

Finally, remember to thank the candidate for her time. Ask her if she has any questions and explain the next steps in your hiring process.

- "Michelle, thank you for meeting with us today. Before you leave, do you have any additional questions for us about the job? Does the job sound like it is what you are looking for? We are interviewing two other people and will be following up by calling each person's references. Before we hire we will be setting up an interview in our home, so candidates can meet our children."

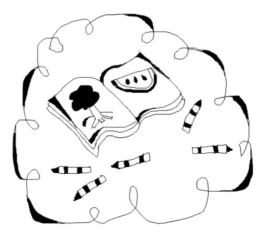

What if Your Caregiver Wants to Bring Her Child to Work?

Would you consider hiring a caregiver who brought her child with her to work? Before turning away an otherwise wonderful candidate you might want to examine the circumstances.

How much care would her child require? How old is the child? Care for an infant is more time-consuming than supervising a four-year-old.

Would the child come with the caregiver every workday? Only part of the day? Only during school vacations?

How compatible is her child with your child(ren)? Do you have a five-year-old who is eager to have a similar age playmate?

Several positive outcomes are possible.

A friendly, school-aged child who visits during school vacation may become a treasured visitor to your preschool child.

An only child will have the opportunity to learn to share, negotiate, and appreciate the differences of others.

Two five-year-olds will entertain themselves for hours playing dress-up, freeing the caregiver to attend to your infant.

Potential difficulties include:

Decreased attention to your child by the caregiver.

Increased wear and tear on your home. The more children, the more potential damage.

Differences in rules. The behavioral expectations must meet your standards.

Undesirable behaviors or lack of compatibility with your child(ren). You can't just say "Michael can't come over to play anymore."

Checking references is a necessary step in the hiring process. Former employers will be able to tell you if your candidate's behavior matches her presentation of herself. A wonderful employee who is no longer needed will have an employer who is eager to help her find a good position. In situations that were less than ideal, you may find a former employer reluctant to speak candidly about the candidate's weaknesses. Specific questions about the employee's activities will provide more information than general questions.

"Hello, my name is Tom Smith. I was given your name as reference for Marie Fiero. She has applied for a job with us as a nanny. Do you have time to talk right now, or would another time be better?"

"When did Marie work for you? Would you describe her duties? How many children did Marie care for, and what were their ages during her time with you?"

"What types of activities did she do with your child(ren)? What was her relationship like with the child(ren)? Did she communicate daily with you on the child(ren)'s behavior and activities? What was her style of discipline? Did you problem-solve together when challenges arose?"

"What are Marie's strengths? What are her weaknesses? If you could have changed one thing about her, what would it have been?"

"Why is she no longer in your employment? Would you hire her again? I'd like to leave my name and phone number, if you think of anything else I should know, please don't hesitate to call."

A few open-ended questions can be useful too. For example, "Can you talk a little bit about her reliability – times she may have been late or absent?"

In addition to checking references, you should consider getting a copy of the candidate's driving record and check that she has no criminal background. Contact your local Department of Motor Vehicles and police station for procedures. A more complete investigation into the background of a potential caregiver can be provided by a detective agency. Check in the yellow pages of your phone book for agencies in your area.

The Second Interview

The primary goal of the second interview is to observe the candidate's interaction with your child(ren). A person who will be caring for an infant should make eye contact with the baby, talk to the baby in a pleasant voice, and watch for the baby's cues that he is interested in interaction. A wonderful caregiver for a toddler and preschooler will make eye contact with the child, kneel down to their level, call them by name, and show interest in what they are doing. An outgoing child will immediately respond and show the person her room and all her favorite toys. A more watchful child will stay near her parent and check out the potential caregiver. The person you want will be respectful of the child and follow her cues of availability during this first interaction.

In addition to meeting your child(ren), you will want to show the candidate around the house. An applicant for a live-in position will be particularly interested in the caregiver's quarters and set up. If you are providing a car for your caregiver, you will want to give her an opportunity to operate the car with you as a passenger. After a brief discussion of the features of the automobile, direct the caregiver to a place she will frequent if hired (i.e., preschool, a park, doctor's office).

Red Flags

Lateness for interview.

Inappropriate appearance.

Lack of eye contact.

Asks no questions.

Asks questions only about salary, benefits, hours.

Expresses interest in a job in another field.

Talks about a boyfriend.

Has held several jobs for short periods of time.

Doesn't attempt to interact with child(ren).

Grabs your baby without asking your permission.

Several of her references fail to return your phone messages.

You feel unease even though everything appears in order.

Making a Decision

Hopefully, after the first and second interviews you feel you have at least one candidate who will meet your needs. Some families gather additional information by arranging for the candidate to care for the child(ren) for a few hours. Before you make your final decision, ask yourself the following questions:

Does she meet all of our requirements as described in the job description?

Do I feel comfortable having this person in my home?

Does she interact well with all members of the family?

Will this person truly care about the well-being of my children?

Does this person have the maturity to handle the day-to-day challenges of young children?

Are her ideas about discipline similar to my own?

Is she easy to talk with?

Is she willing to bring up concerns and also open to working with me to determine possible solutions?

Do I feel comfortable leaving my child(ren) in her care?

Hiring

When you make an offer, you may want to present a formal work agreement that includes the duties and responsibilities of the job, the terms of employment, and your obligations as the employer. Begin the hiring process with a call to the candidate, expressing your desire for her to fill your position. Briefly describe the offer, the wage rate, starting date, and benefits. Indicate that you will be sending a copy of the work agreement in the mail for her review and that you look forward to speaking with her in detail about the offer once she has had a chance to review it. Once the agreement is signed, both parties should retain a copy for their files. Some families find a work agreement too formal and choose to hire in-home care on looser terms. You need to determine your own comfort level.

Putting Together a Work Agreement

The work agreement consists of two parts, the job description and a statement of terms. Review the job description you developed as you were defining your needs. After talking with potential caregivers you may see areas you wish to revise. Be sure the responsibilities and duties accurately and specifically reflect your expectations of the caregiver. The statement of terms you create will address work schedule, compensation, performance reviews, and termination issues. Personalize the following Statement of Terms to meet your unique situation. If your agreement includes tax-withholding, you'll want to have a W-4 form available with the work agreement.

Statement of Terms

Employee name _____

Employer name _____

Start date _____

WORK SCHEDULE

Hours of child care to be provided each week _____

Scheduled work hours are from _____ to _____ Monday through Friday.

Overtime hours will be scheduled as mutually agreed by both parties.

COMPENSATION

Weekly rate of pay _____ Payable on _____

Overtime will be accounted and paid in the following manner:

Employer will withhold all required state and federal taxes (Social Security taxes, Medicare, unemployment tax, worker's compensation insurance) from the employee's salary. The employee may choose to have employer withhold state and federal income taxes or make quarterly payments themselves.

I   do ☐   don't ☐   want the employer to withhold income taxes.

BENEFITS TO BE PAID BY EMPLOYER

Live-in Accommodations (if applicable):

The following will be provided for your comfort:

Permission must be obtained from the employer before any changes are made to the room including: painting, changing the wall covering, drilling holes, and any other alterations that may cause permanent changes. Any damage that occurs to the room and its contents due to negligence or misconduct will be the responsibility of the caregiver.

Statement of Terms CONTINUED

JOB PERFORMANCE AND PAY REVIEW

Job performance evaluation will occur at the end of the first month of employment. Thereafter, job performance and salary review will occur once a year. (Though you hope to have an open relationship with your caregiver so that either one of you feels comfortable addressing any issue at any time.)

TERMINATION OF AGREEMENT

At this time both parties contemplate that employment will continue at least one year. Either party can terminate the agreement without notice during the first thirty days. After that date, each party agrees to give the other three weeks' notice of termination. If employer is unable to give three weeks' notice, three weeks' severance pay will be provided. If termination is the result of gross negligence or misconduct, the caregiver will be immediately terminated, and one week's severance pay will given.

   Both parties mutually agree to the conditions described in the Statement of Terms and the attached Job Description. The signed Statement of Terms and Job Description constitute our Work Agreement.

Employee signature _____ Date _____

Employer signature _____ Date _____

Off-the-Books Payment Issues

After an exhaustive search you've found a wonderful nanny, a person who was highly recommended by her previously family. A stumbling block in her hiring is her request to be paid off the books. Before you consent to her request consider the following:

- Form 1040 on your taxes specifically asks if you employ household help. Failing to report payroll taxes compromises the integrity of your tax return. If you are caught paying "under the table" you will be liable for back taxes, penalties, and interest. There is no statue of limitations on the failure to report payroll taxes.

You find the thought of keeping payroll records and filing the appropriate tax forms overwhelming. You are hiring a caregiver to make your life simpler, not more complex. Before you succumb to the positive features of paying off the books, consider the possible negative outcomes which include:

- If your caregiver attempts to collect unemployment or Social Security benefits at some future time, you will have to pay back taxes, penalties, and interest.

- Tax breaks are available for child or dependent care only if your child care provider is paid legally.

- A caregiver who has worked all her life loving and nurturing other people's children will enter retirement with no Social Security benefits of her own to support her.

- Paying off the books may compromise your desire to have a caregiver who is a professional.

CHAPTER 3

Getting Acquainted

Y ou've hired a child care provider, now try to put yourself in her shoes and imagine you were stepping into your house without knowing much about the family, the home, and, possibly, the community. What will she need to be successful? Prior to that first day alone with the children, you and the care provider should try to schedule a block of time to "walk through the day" and "walk through the house." This orientation session should contain important information including a description of your child(ren)'s favorites, current challenges, good friends, daily schedule, safety rules and procedures and house rules. Your caregiver will appreciate a written record of the orientation information that she can keep handy for future reference. For an example of a Personalized Caregiver's Book, turn to the Appendix.

Introductions

While your nanny may have a lot of experience with children, she will need to get to know your child(ren). You can help her by sharing the following types of information.

Favorites: Starting very early in life children show preference for particular items, songs and activities. While favorites change over time they continue to be very important to children. For many children a favorite blanket or stuffed animal helps them feel secure during times of stress (i.e., change of routine or caregiver).

Growing Pains: Children's bodies are growing and developing, creating new and exciting challenges for both child and caregiver. Sharing your child's current challenges and strategies will help ease your child's transition to her new caregiver. For example:

> "Nine-month-old McKena is learning to pull up to standing, sometimes during her nap I find her standing in her crib crying. She hasn't learned how to get down yet. When I calmly lay her back down she goes right back to sleep."

> "Two-and-a-half-year-old Steven is working very hard on becoming an independent person. If you say, "Steven it is time to go inside for lunch" he will say "No." If, however, you say "Steven, I'll race you inside for lunch" or "Let's pretend were riding motorcycles inside to lunch" you'll be on your way."

> "Three-year-old Ali is just beginning to be interested in using the potty. She wears panties during the day, and we are helping her to recognize that when she crosses her legs that it's a sign that she needs to go. Keep an eye on her and when you see the cue say 'I see you have your legs crossed, would you like to go sit on the potty?'

> "Four-year-old Sarah is afraid of dogs. Please respect her fear and don't force her to be near any dogs."

Welcome to Our Community

A caregiver new to the community will appreciate the following:

- *A good map.*

- *Suggestions for dentist, doctors, and other health care providers.*

- *Locations of banks, post office, hairdresser, and grocery stores.*

- *Directions to library, parks, shopping centers, movie theater, and places of worship.*

- *Information about local community activities, cultural events, and places of interest.*

- *The local newspaper.*

- *A local parenting newspaper, if available.*

- **Routines:** Repeating the same procedures often at the same time of day helps children feel secure and reduces the number of conflicts during the day. What are your child(ren)'s routines? For example:

"Three-year-old Jennifer gets three small animal cookies after lunch every day because she is three. Two-year-old Tommy always listens to the same music when he goes for his nap, the door is left open just an inch and he needs his blanket with the truck on it. Six-year-old Andrew eats an apple and watches one half-hour of television before he goes outside to play after school."

- **Mischief and Misbehavior:** What problems are you and your child(ren) currently experiencing? Sibling squabbles, picky eating, refusing to nap, potty training issues, tantrums, and refusing to pick up their bedroom are a few common problems. Share these with your caregiver. Don't forget to tell her what solution you are hoping for, and what has worked and not worked for you in these situations. You might also want to ask for her ideas.

- **Thoughts on Health and Medicine:** Obviously, you will want to be very thorough in explaining procedures for any child with special needs. Don't assume anything. If your caregiver will be giving your child medication, explain exactly how and when it is to be given. Give your caregiver in writing all the information that they will need in a medical emergency, including your contact numbers, doctor's numbers, and directions to the nearest emergency room.

First Aid, Emergencies, and Accidents

1. Determine if it is life threatening. If yes, call 911 immediately.
2. For bumps, scrapes, and minor hurts, please administer the appropriate first aid and lots of love.
3. If it is not life threatening, but more than a minor hurt, call a parent immediately.

    Dad's daytime number _____

    Mom's daytime number _____

4. If a parent is not available, call the child's doctor.

    Children's doctor _____

    Phone number _____

    Address _____

    Insurance Policy # _____

In addition to getting to know your child(ren), your caregiver will likely need to be made aware of, and introduced to, other significant people and animals in your household.

- **Household Help:** Explain to your caregiver the responsibilities and schedule of any other household employees. Make sure she has the opportunity to meet each person.

- **Pets:** Be sure that your caregiver has met all the family's pets. Clarify the rules regarding pets, both the rules that protect the child and those that protect the pet. Remember, if you have any expectations for the caregiver regarding the pet, be sure to make these known from the beginning.

- **Significant Family Members:** You'll want to consider variations to the daily routine. Will your mother be dropping by occasionally to see her grandchildren? Do your children have a favorite aunt who occasionally takes them for an ice cream cone in the afternoon? Your caregiver will need to know who is allowed to visit and entertain the children.

- **Children's Friends:** Who are your children's friends, and their friends' parents. It's important to describe for your caregiver who is allowed to come to your home to play and when your child is allowed to visit another child's home.

- **Neighbors:** Do you have some neighbors who you can count on in case of an emergency? In addition to introducing your caregiver to your neighbors, be sure your caregiver has the name, address, and phone number of these important contacts.

Schedule

What are your expectations for the time your caregiver spends with your child(ren)? Your caregiver needs to know these right from the start. Remember to begin with her arrival, include how the transition from parent to caregiver will be made, include all activities the caregiver is to perform during your time away and, finally, describe the transition at the end of the day.

PLANNING THE DAY

Morning Transition

- Your workday begins at 8:00 A.M.
- The boys are usually still in their PJs looking at books.
- I will leave around 8:15, and will want to speak briefly with you before I leave.
- Begin preparing the boys' breakfast to be eaten at 8:30.
- Following breakfast, the boys are to get dressed, brush their hair and teeth. Peter will need help with brushing his teeth and hair.

Daytime Activities

- Take boys outside sometime during the day. Current favorite outside activities include: drawing with sidewalk chalk, walking to the park, and walking to the post office to drop off the mail.

- Read to the boys at least several times a day, and as much as possible.
- Limit television viewing to one hour during the day. A list of appropriate programs is posted on the refrigerator.
- Lunch should be eaten between 12:00 and 12:30 (or, if you allow your child to choose meal times, let your nanny know too). Available lunch foods will be listed on the refrigerator door. The boys are to wash their hands before eating and all food is to be eaten at the table.
- Afternoon snack consists of cheese, juice, and fruit.
- Both boys are to have a quiet time after their snack in the afternoon at 3:30. Peter will sleep. Joshua needs to stay in his room, looking at books or playing with his toys quietly for at least thirty minutes.

Evening Transition

- At least one parent will be home by 5:30.
- That parent will greet the boys, speak with you about your day and then go change clothes.
- Your workday ends at 6:00 P.M. Please develop a goodbye ritual with the children and also let the parent know you are leaving.

Home Tour

During the interview, your caregiver got her first view of your home. The orientation tour will focus on specifics. Consider the following:

- Where your caregiver can store her caregiving supplies and personal items.

- Areas, equipment, and furniture that are not available for caregiver or child(ren)'s use.

- How the security system works and what to do if she accidentally pushes the wrong button.

- How to operate the washer and dryer, heating and air-conditioning systems, vacuum cleaner, television, stereo, telephone, and answering machine.

- Location of the fuse box, flashlights, and water cut-off valve in case of an emergency.

- Procedures for answering the phone and taking messages.

- Location of important items in the kitchen including your child(ren)'s favorite spoon and cup; favorite cereal, cookies, and other foods; plastic wrap and storage containers, garbage, fire extinguisher, and cleaning supplies.

- Exactly how you prepare your infant's formula or breast milk.

- *How to use kitchen equipment such as the microwave and dishwasher.*

- *Your expectations for cleanup after child(ren)'s meals.*

- *Procedures for developing grocery lists.*

- *Where you keep cash for outings and supplies and how you want your caregiver to account for her purchases. To determine the amount of cash to make available, consider the types of activities you want your caregiver to provide for your child(ren).*

- *Diapering procedures, supplies, and safety.*

- *Rules and expectations about picking up living areas, child(ren)'s bedrooms, and bathrooms.*

- *Room-by-room description of safety trouble spots, childproofing efforts, and prevention strategies. Don't forget to include any outside play areas in your tour.*

Every family has rules regarding the care and use of their home. Your caregiver will appreciate knowing these rules up front, thus avoiding possible misunderstandings. Some examples include:

- No visitors without prior consent from a parent.

- No grape juice outside the kitchen.

- Take off your shoes before coming inside.

- Turn off lights when a room is not being used.

- Keep the stairway clear of clutter at all times.

- No climbing on living room furniture.

- Markers and clay can be used at crafts table only.

- The dog is not allowed on the second floor.

- Hang coats in the closet or on the hooks in the laundry room.

- Finger painting is an outside activity.

- Children are not to place their fingers on the television screen.

- Children may build forts with chairs and blankets. No sofa cushions are to be used for fort building.

- Always hang wet towels and clothes in the bathroom to dry.

Our Story

"With respect to housekeeping issues (i.e., vacuuming, kitchen cleanup, laundry, etc.) I recommend that you show the caregiver exactly what you want done and how you want it done. Follow up with an exhaustive list recounting your expectations. For example, it may seem ridiculous, but you should show the caregiver exactly which cleaners you want used on various surfaces. I would also make it very clear that the children are first and that any housecleaning duties are second."

CHAPTER 4

Partners from the Start

> Mutual respect and trust develop over time as parents and caregiver work together to meet the challenges of raising children.

No two people think and work alike. The differences between successful and unsuccessful child care arrangements often hinge on the willingness of both parties to identify problems, communicate effectively, and stay focused on solutions. Mutual respect and trust develop over time as parents and caregiver work together to meet the challenges of raising children.

Good Relationships

Try to remember that in high-quality child care arrangements the role, responsibilities, and needs of each person are clear and respected. The parent is the most important person in the child(ren)'s life. While the parent seeks the input of others working with her child(ren), ultimately she is responsible for providing an environment that protects, nurtures, and supports the growth of her children. It's important that the caregiver understands that her role is to provide safe, loving, and stimulating care in the absence of the parent and according to the parent's instructions.

Mutual support is a crucial element in good caregiving relationships. The parent may think that the caregiver's insistence that her son put away the crayons before lunch is unnecessary, however, she should try to stay out of the interaction, asking the caregiver about it privately only if the interaction seems inappropriate. Allowing the caregiver to be different is difficult for many people. While you may wish your caregiver would do a better job putting the dishes away when emptying the dishwasher, you are thrilled with her willingness to play pretend with your daughter for hours on end. Consider that in successful relationships both parent and caregiver stay focused on the positive and have learned to let the little things go. There is always compromise in relationships, and learning to pick your issues is an important skill.

How to Be a Good Supervisor

Building relationships requires good management skills. While you may initially be uncomfortable in your role as an employer, it is imperative that you view this role as important. Your caregiver expects direction and it is leadership that your child(ren) desire. Remember the goal: Building a strong relationship to provide consistent, quality care for your family.

A Good Supervisor:

1. Pays on time.
2. Clearly communicates expectations.
3. Establishes communication strategies.
4. Provides regular feedback.
5. Asks for and values employee input.
6. Gets home on time.
7. Apologizes when wrong.
8. Is respectful of employee boundaries.
9. Takes time to "chat."
10. Deals with issues in a timely manner.
11. Supports the caregiver's relationship with the child.
12. Identifies problems and focuses on solutions.
13. Is familiar with the law and liabilities of employing the caregiver.
14. Is consistent in the statement and enforcement of rules.
15. Gives status and "ownership" to the employee.

Reliable, nurturing caregivers become more than just valued employees, they become part of the family. In addition to having spent many hours together sharing the milestones and the challenges of growth, you may meet and share meals with her family, and friends, help her solve personal problems, and share similar interests. As the comfort level of the relationship increases, it is important that both parent and caregiver respect each other's time and needs and not take advantage of the relationship. For example, while your caregiver might be available to care for your child occasionally in the evening, be sure to ask well in advance and provide extra pay for those hours. All relationships need boundaries and having an employee in your home can test these boundaries. Clearly thought-out house rules and regular communication will go a long way toward reducing misunderstandings and frustration.

You have hired a caregiver to give you time. Obviously, however a quality child care relationship requires a significant amount of your time, particularly in the beginning. Children thrive in care situations that are loving, consistent, and stimulating. You need to view this time as an investment in your child(ren)'s future.

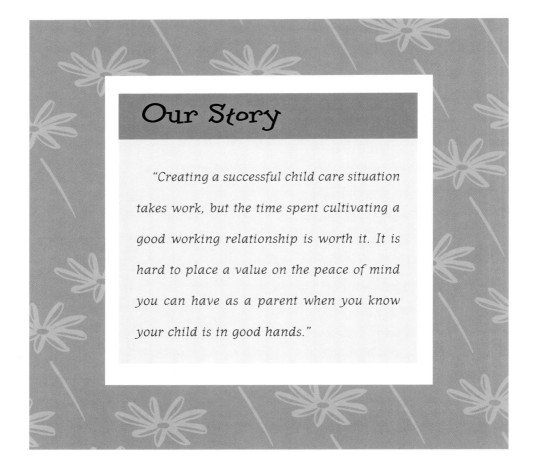

Our Story

"Creating a successful child care situation takes work, but the time spent cultivating a good working relationship is worth it. It is hard to place a value on the peace of mind you can have as a parent when you know your child is in good hands."

From the start of your relationship with the caregiver, you need to establish both formal and informal patterns of communication. Telling your caregiver to "Please come to me with any concerns or questions you have about the children and the household" is not enough. Without regular communication, a small problem that you or your caregiver didn't take the time to mention can become a huge problem and could result in hurt feelings or a damaged relationship.

What is the best time for you to touch bases with your caregiver? A telephone call during nap time, or a shared cup of tea once parents have arrived home are two strategies families use. You may find the question "How was your day?" all you need to open a comfortable conversation about the activities of the day. Not all caregivers, however, are comfortable talking with their employers in the beginning. Sometimes, you will need to ask specific questions "How long did Sam cry after I left?"; "Did Ron fuss today at nap time?"; "Did Madison talk about the bad dream she had last night?" The question "What was the best and worst thing that happened today?" often provides insight into your caregiver's and your children's day.

In addition to everyday chats, some families use a written log. Having your caregiver keep a written account of the day serves several purposes. First, it offers a quick update on your child(ren)'s day. For example, if you know that Rebecca (who is usually a happy child) woke up grumpy from her nap, you may keep an eye on her to see if she is coming down with something. Knowing that Matthew ate very little will affect the foods you offer him later that evening.

Second, a written log provides an opportunity for the caregiver to evaluate the day. After a full day of toddler "no's," sibling conflicts, and picky eating, taking a few quiet minutes to reflect on the day, its challenges and successes, helps identify what is working and helps solve recurring problems.

Finally, consider that this written record gives both parent and caregiver valuable information as they look for patterns of behavior and try to solve problems. Patricia's mom and nanny found the log invaluable when they went to address Patricia's finicky eating. Both were concerned Patricia wasn't getting enough to eat. A quick look at the log for the previous week revealed that, while she indeed had meals where she ate lightly, she seemed to catch up by eating big meals every few days. Sue and her nanny decided to use the log as a tool to track two-year-old Joshua's tantrums. Both recorded the time of day Joshua threw a tantrum, and what the tantrum was about, for a period of one week. Using the information gained from their record keeping, Sue and her nanny developed a strategy for preventing Joshua's tantrums—then used the log to record its effectiveness.

You will want to personalize the log to reflect the developmental challenges of your child(ren). As the parent of an infant, you will want to know about feeding, elimination, and sleep periods. If you are the parent of a toddler who is learning to use the potty, you will likely want to know about attempts and successes. For a kindergartener who is having trouble with the transition to school, it is helpful to know how his first hour home from school went. It's important for all parties that you emphasis to your caregiver that specific statements like "The first thing Micah said when he came home was that he made a friend, he was very excited and told me that he couldn't wait until tomorrow when he could play with Zak at recess," give you more information than "Micah had a good day today at school."

Not all caregivers will welcome the request to complete the daily log. Depending on the number of children, it can be seen as a burden. Designing your daily log so that it is easy to fill out will help reduce the time commitment on the caregiver's part. An example of a daily log is shown in the Personalized Caregiver's Book at the end of the text. It's important that you explain to your caregiver how important and valid her observations are to you and how together you will be able to face the important developmental changes and challenges that all children experience. As your caregiver gets accustomed to using the log, try to ask for her input on helpful information to record. This respect for her opinions will enhance both your relationship and the development of your children.

Make Plans to Meet

In the beginning, you may want to schedule meetings on a weekly basis. Once your caregiver becomes comfortable with the child(ren) and the household routines and you have established a daily two-way dialogue, monthly meetings will likely be enough. Remember these are the scheduled discussions. Don't forget to emphasize that less formal discourse remains important.

How to Address Your Concerns

Here are some strategies to raise issues that are on your mind—and to have good interactions with your care-provider:

- **You want to know what your caregiver is thinking**
  "Marion, I know that this first week has been a very busy one for you. I'm eager to hear your observations on how the children are adjusting, and about any concerns you have."

- **You're worried about your child's behavior**
  "I have noticed that Morgan has been fixed on fighting bad guys in his pretend play this week. Yesterday he was pretending that a large block was a gun and he was shooting at bad guys. Does he play like this during the day also? While I think it's important for children to have the opportunity to work out their fears in pretend play, I'm concerned about. . ."

- **Checking in on progress**
  "I've been wondering how Michele is doing with sharing? Last time we talked you mentioned that she was having a lot of trouble letting Hillary play with her toys when she came over. Did it help when you had Michele put away a few of her most precious items before Hillary came over?"

- **Solving problems together**
  "Thank you so much for mentioning your concern about Nathan's use of cursing. It caught us by surprise yesterday when we heard him. I agree with you that we need to decide together on a way to respond when he uses inappropriate words. What ideas do you have for handling the situation?"

- **Growing-up phases**
  "Haley will be six months old next week. Her doctor has said that she can start solid foods and gave me this information about signs of readiness. I made this copy for you. I thought I would offer her some rice cereal on Saturday and see how it goes. I'll let you know how it went and what the plan is on Monday."

- **Offering praise**
  "Hanna has been singing the Swedish songs you taught her. She is really excited to know some actual Swedish words and is giving her dad some lessons. I think that's great."

- **Upcoming events**

  "In two weeks, Caley only has school half days as the teachers are holding parent-teacher conferences. How do you think that will affect Nick? He is used to having you all to himself until late afternoon."

- **Contract issues**

  "According to your contract you are entitled to two weeks of vacation. I'm wondering if you have given any thought to when you wanted to take that time. While the contract states that we need two weeks notice, as soon as you firm up your plans I'd appreciate knowing."

- **Household rules**

  "Yesterday when I went into the children's bathroom I found a pile of wet towels. It's really important that they get hung up so that they will dry. Would it help if we put some hooks at child height in the laundry room so that the towels could be hung up immediately upon coming in the house from playing in the water outside?"

- **Scheduling Problems**

  "On Tuesdays I have a meeting that gets over at 6:00, I know that when I'm not home by 6:30 you have to hustle to get to your class. I have a couple ideas about how to make this transition work better and still have both of us get where we need to go. I'd like to hear you thoughts on these and hear any ideas you have."

- **Live-In Issues**

  "Have you noticed how stuffed the refrigerator has been lately? When I went through all the little containers of food I found some that were long past edible. We need to come up with a system of labeling and clearing out containers that will allow us to better utilize the food that is in there and free up some space."

Au Pair's Story

"From the first moment, they showed me and told me that I would be a part of the family as their au pair. They never made me feel like I would interrupt them or destroy their privacy when I stayed home when I was not working. We went together to family gatherings, we went out for dinner or we spent a holiday together in the Natural Museum of History. I enjoyed all these activities during my "time off" very, very much and they always made me feel like I was a part of the family."

Our Story

"Marianne is like a part of our family, yet she is still an employee of our household. Recognizing this dichotomy is important. For instance, I have gotten in trouble a couple times when I forgot to consider that caring for my children is her job—not just a pleasure. In other words, to have a successful relationship with an in-home caregiver, one must walk a fine line. That line is defined on one side by being warm, welcoming, and open with your caregiver, and defined on the other side by requiring that you respect the caregiver's boundaries (i.e., their scheduled times, their time off, etc.)."

Today when you came home from work your daughter was wearing her "Minnie" dress, the same "Minnie" dress she wore yesterday and the day before that. Why, you wonder, did the nanny let her wear it again today. She has a whole closet full of clothes. After three days that dress must be filthy. Another thing you've noticed is that in the last week your daughter has been having trouble getting to sleep at night, she's up until 11:00 P.M. and you're exhausted by then. For months she's been a regular sleeper, down by 8:30. Concerns and differences in parenting are inevitable, even in the most successful parent/caregiver relationships.

First, ask yourself "If I allow the nanny to continue her approach to this situation, will my child be harmed?" A full-time nanny is on the firing line all day with your children. Daily communication about the ins and outs of your child's day will give you a better appreciation of the reasoning behind your caregiver's choices. She may have decided that fighting over clothing choice with your two and a half year old was a battle she wasn't going to pick. By allowing your daughter to wear her Minnie dress, your nanny has found the day gets off to a good start. Two and a half year olds are becoming their own person and having favorites and wanting to make choices is very important. Together the two of you can decide a way to get the dress clean, just in case it is selected as the garment of choice tomorrow.

One thing to remember is that compromise often is the best solution for occasional clashes in opinions. In casual discussion about your daughter's day you have learned that she has begun taking two-hour naps in the late afternoon. Your nanny is quite happy about the development, since your daughter had previously not been napping in the afternoon. Now she wakes from her nap happy and has fewer tantrums then before the naps. What works for your nanny during the day is obviously causing you problems at bedtime. Insisting that your nanny not let your daughter take a late afternoon nap is not the answer here. Remember the goal is not to win but to identify common concerns and focus on what's in the best interest of the child. Together you and your nanny can brainstorm solutions, select a strategy, and then give each other feedback on how the approach is working.

At other times, you will need to step in and clearly state your position as the parent. This approach is called for whenever your child's health and safety are at risk. "Tommy must have his bike helmet on whenever he rides his trike, we have that rule for his safety and I expect you to enforce it."

When you have a tough talk, try to:

Be calm.

Avoid "you" statements.

Be clear about your concern.

Avoid placing blame.

Listen to the caregiver's perspective.

Focus on problems and solutions.

The Caregiver's Perspective

"When I have an ongoing problem with a child, for example a two year old who runs in the street, I approach the parents by saying "I'm worried about Camille, she runs in the street when we are outside and she won't listen to me. Can we work together to decide how to approach the problem?"

An Au Pair's Perspective

"It was hard for me to accept that not everything I did in my job and as a part of the family was right and that there would be misunderstandings. But I have the opinion that I am the "new one" in the family and I have to accept reasonable criticism and try to change or do things in a different way. I wanted to do everything right so I didn't want to argue about small disagreements. I accepted their opinions in most cases."

Keeping Her Happy

Three-and-a-half-year-old Mike refused to use the potty today, he insisted on wearing pull-ups, he threw his lunch on the floor because he wanted bow tie noodles, not macaroni and cheese, and when Matthew, his brother, refused to share a toy car with him, he had a tantrum for twenty minutes. As a parent you know that some days are like that, in fact, some weeks are like that. "No I won't, It's mine!" and "I do it!" are all parts of normal development. Children can wear down even the most loving care providers. A long time can pass between big hugs, toothless smiles, and specially crafted pictures.

As parents, we should consider that it is in our own best interest to acknowledge how tough caring for our children can be. Without positive feedback your care provider will begin to feel frustrated and unappreciated. While monetary feedback in the form of raises, bonuses, and gifts are always welcome, nonmonetary feedback can go a long way toward enhancing your caregiver's self-esteem.

Examples of nonmonetary feedback are:

It's important to take notice of the little things she does. "Thank you so much for picking up the blocks. We lost track of the time last night and didn't get it done."

Make an effort daily to talk with your caregiver about the bests and the worst of her day.

Share with her how your son toddles around the house looking for her after she leaves and how he points to her picture on the refrigerator and says, "Im" (Kim).

Try to remember to show interest in her, beyond her caregiving role. Ask how the class she is taking is going or how she liked the movie she saw over the weekend.

Praise your nanny in public. "This is our nanny Michelle, I don't know what I'd do without her, she's terrific!"

Money Talks!

A raise or a bonus is always welcomed by a caregiver. It is standard practice to give a raise after a year of service. Several factors should be considered when determining the amount of the raise.

Raises should at least cover the cost of living and generally fall between 5 to 10 percent of weekly salary.

The amount of a raise is seen by caregivers to reflect your attitude about their value to the family. A generous raise communicates appreciativeness for the work she does.

Lavish spending on children, furnishings, and vacations followed by a small caregiver raise will likely result in a poor attitude and frequent turnover.

After receiving generous raises several years in a row, your caregiver's salary may far exceed the local market rate. At some point you may need to give smaller raises and provide other incentives such as bonuses and gifts.

A bonus or one time gift of money is given for different reasons. Some families give a bonus to acknowledge a caregiver's birthday and the holidays. Other families provide incentive for their caregiver to stay in their service by offering a bonus after each year of service.

An Au Pair's Story

"I am lucky to work for a caring, considerate family. From the start they have respected my time by not showing up late or calling at the last minute to let me know they had to work late. Since I go to school at night it's really important that I leave on time. The other day, Susan, the mom, told Jacob that he was really lucky to have an au pair who loves him and could build amazing forts. At that moment her comments felt especially good. It had been a tough day, keeping a four year old entertained and at the same time caring for a baby with a bad cold. This year on Valentine's Day, Susan and Jacob made a big heart cookie for me and decorated it with Jacob's favorite colors, purple and orange. On my birthday, they gave me a surprise birthday party and Jacob presented me with a bouquet of flowers from the garden he and I planted. Since I have no family in the area, the thoughtfulness of "my other family" has made this job a joy."

With careful thought and planning you found the right caregiver, now it is time to use those skills to make your caregiving back-up plan. Two types of situations, vacation or illness, are likely to occur. The easiest to plan for is when your caregiver gives you advance notice according to the work agreement that she will be taking vacation or a personal day. A more difficult situation is when your caregiver is unable to work due to illness, injury, or a personal emergency. In making your back-up plan, consider the following:

- Can you care for the child(ren)? If you have plenty of notice? No notice? Can you work from home? Can you provide care part of the day?

- Do you have any family members who are available to fill in?

- Are there any friends who are home with their children, who might be willing to fill-in in a pinch? Or friends who might be willing to share their caregiver?

- Do you have any neighbors who might be able to help? A retired woman who has befriended your children might be willing to step in and help?

- Who do you know who has high school or college-aged children who might be available during summer or school vacations?

- Does your caregiver have a family member or friend who could provide back-up care?

- Is there a quality preschool or child care center nearby which your child could attend?

Take time now to nurture relationships between your back-up providers and your child(ren). It is much easier for a child to cope with the change in routine when she knows and trusts the person who will be caring for her.

Change in Circumstances

No child care situation lasts forever. A relationship with a caregiver who is a part of the family often ends when circumstances change. As children enter school, a family's need for child care often changes. A move due to a job change, or addition of a new baby commonly affect the need for child care. Caregiver's lives change also, they return to school, marry and start a family, and decide to try a different career. If you are the one initiating the separation, be clear in your reason for the change, and when the change will happen. Provide plenty of notice so that your caregiver has enough time to find another situation, and offer your assistance in helping her find another job. And remember, your caregiver is not just losing a job, she is losing an important relationship with your child(ren) and your family.

The Occasional Babysitter

Most families have times when they need child care beyond their regular child care schedule. The tendency for many families is to depend on their primary caregiver for these occasions. Some individuals will welcome the extra pay that comes with the extra hours, while others cherish their off time. If your caregiver is full-time, the time away from children is necessary for them to recoup and refresh for the challenges of the next day. A babysitter who will care for your children on a time-to-time basis can be found in several places. Begin by asking friends and neighbors who they use to babysit. Also check neighborhood bulletin boards, young people who are interested in babysitting often use these to advertise their services. Churches and preschools are other good locations for connecting with people who enjoy children. And, finally, check with your caregiver, she may have a friend or family member who may be happy to help you out.

Parting with a Loved One

Jennifer, blanket in hand, waits and watches at the window every morning for Nicole to come. When Nicole arrives they hug and then race to say good morning to the dolls and stuffed animals in Jennifer's room. Then with at least one stuffed animal, Nicole with Jennifer on piggy-back comes to wave goodbye and sends her parents on their way for the day. The security of having a loving caregiver and daily routines is very important to children. Losing a much-loved caregiver such as Nicole is difficult for most children. Try to recognize that for many children this will be their first significant loss. A change in caregiver also means a change in daily routine.

The response to the loss will depend both on the age of the child and the unique personality of the child. Normal responses for young children who have difficult using words to express their emotions may include whining, clinging and withdrawing. Parents may find children regress to previous behaviors, bed wetting, thumb-sucking and nightmares. Older children will often express anger at one of the parties "How can you leave me!" "Why are you letting her go?"

Ways you can help ease this difficult time for children include:

Try to explain clearly that your caregiver will not be coming to care for them any longer. "Mommy is going to stay home with you and Teresa is not going to be coming any more." "Since you will be in school during the day, Monica will not be coming to our house. She is going to a new family to take care of a baby, just like she did when you were a baby." "Nina is going to be having a baby of her own. She is going to be busy taking care of the new baby and won't be able to come to our house any more." Some children will worry that the caregiver is leaving because of something they did or that the caregiver doesn't love them anymore. You can calm these fears by letting your children know why the caregiver is leaving, how much you care for the caregiver and how wonderful it has been to have the caregiver as a part of your family.

Talk with your caregiver about ways that she and your child can keep in touch. This way, when you tell your child the caregiver is leaving, you will be able to say "Even though we won't see Teresa like we used to, you will still be able to talk with her on the phone and we will send her notes with your picture in it so she can see how much you have grown." Some families continue to use their caregiver for occasional babysitting, and others arrange dates with the caregiver. Many families who have become attached to an au pair plan to visit her in her country.

Children of all ages are affected by how their parents and caregiver respond to the change. If you are anxious, harried, and unavailable, your children may feel insecure and frightened. During a change children often wonder, "Who will care for me? Will everyone leave me?" When parents are calm, patient and available for extra cuddles, a child can learn to feel secure in his ability to deal with the change.

It's important to consider how this change will affect your child(ren)'s schedule.

Will he wake up at the same time? What about meals, naps, story time, and other routine activities? Changes in schedule can be upsetting and energy depleting for young children. The departure of a loved caregiver will be easier for a child whose life stays the same in as many other ways as possible.

By celebrating all the good feelings and times you had with your caregiver, you serve two purposes. It helps both the child and the caregiver (and you too) work through their feelings of loss. Families have come up with several ways to say goodbye including memory books, videos, and posters. Some families have a going-away party, others plan the last day with the caregiver to include places and activities that have become special over time. When a caregiver is leaving by train or airplane, accompanying her and waving goodbye provide closure for children.

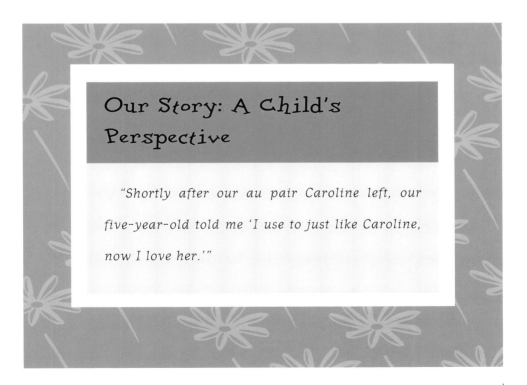

Our Story: A Child's Perspective

"Shortly after our au pair Caroline left, our five-year-old told me 'I use to just like Caroline, now I love her.'"

CHAPTER 5

Challenges

You may be confronted with several challenges on your journey to finding and keeping the best child care. It's best to be aware of these and confront them proactively, rather than have them affect your relationship with your caregiver. Common concerns early in parent-caregiver relationships include "Will my child like the caregiver better than me?" and "How will I know if my caregiver is taking good care of my children?" And then, when everything is working well, you might have to address the issues of caregiver absence whether it be for vacation or illness. Ultimately circumstances will change. Your needs may change or shortcomings may develop in the existing relationship. Your family and the caregiver will part. For some, not finding the right caregiver will put them in the position of having to fire their present caregiver and beginning the process over.

Ambivalent Feelings

You've hired a wonderful caregiver—reliable, loving, and skilled at caring for your children and your children love her. It's great, right? While you are pleased that your children are in such good hands you can't help wondering if they would rather spend their time with her than you. It's possible that occasionally you may feel inadequate as a parent as you marvel at how creative and patient your caregiver is. These feeling could be fueled by statements from children like "Go away, we're playing a game," "I want Vivian to dress me!," "Maria's peanut butter sandwiches are way better than yours!," "Jessica builds the best forts." It is normal for parents to feel a pang of jealousy as they watch the relationship between their child(ren) and caregiver grow. Jealousy only becomes a problem when the parent starts to resent the bond between the caregiver and child. Several things can happen:

- It's possible that the parent begins to compete with the caregiver for the child's love. In an effort to be better than the caregiver, a parent may find herself saying yes to every demand the child makes and going out of her way to please. "Oh, Marie gives you two cookies at lunch, well I give three cookies."

Checklist

Signs of a Good Caregiver-Child Relationship

Does your:

- Child's face brighten when the caregiver arrives?
- Child talk enthusiastically about the things that she and the caregiver did together during the day?
- Child look forward to showing your caregiver his new toys?

Does your:

- Caregiver recognize the special characteristics that make your child a unique person?
- Caregiver know when your child is having trouble and provide appropriate support?
- Caregiver talk about the positive moments she has shared with your child during the day?

- No one is perfect, and a jealous parent can become super critical of any imperfection or mistake. Hair styles, eating habits and even silly songs your child loves can all start to drive you crazy. "If I hear that stupid clean-up song one more time I'll scream!"
- Fearing that the caregiver knows best pulls some parents away from the child, allowing the caregiver to make decisions concerning the children. "Martha is so competent, I just decided to let her call the shots."

All these scenarios beg for an alternative. Try to remember that it is in your child's best interest for you to view your caregiver as a supplement to your parenting rather than as a replacement. At birth, children are capable of developing ongoing relationships with a small number of consistent, loving caregivers. These attachments allow him to learn to trust his environment and the people in it. This love and trust serve as the foundation for his later relationships. While you may not be as creative and patient as your caregiver, your intense love for your child should never be discounted. You and your caregiver are different people. You both play a very significant role in your child's life.

Don't forget that as the parent, you are the most important person in your child's life. If you feel shut out of your child's life, examine the cause. If it is due to your caregiver's attitude "I've raised dozens of children, I know what is best" you will need to clarify with the caregiver her role. It is possible that in her previous experiences parents left the childrearing to her and she has assumed you want the same. In your desire to retain an otherwise skilled and competent caregiver don't negotiate away your responsibility as a parent. Parents retain the ultimate duty to care for their children. The caregiver should only aid you in your tasks. Make it clear that her job is to support your relationship with the child, and that you will do the same for her. Consider that together, your unique love as the parent and her experience can complement each other and provide a rich environment for your child. Your caregiver needs your trust, but she and your child look to you for leadership.

Even with the support of the caregiver, some parents feel out of touch with their child's day-to-day adventures. A possible reason a parent feels this way is that it is true. Busy schedules, the cell phone, household chores, and volunteer activities can all intrude into a family's and individual's true goals. It is important to share your family's values and goals with your caregiver. These principles should reflect in your employee's evaluation and in your own family's discussions. Don't forget that staying in touch requires the same organization and dedication to purpose you displayed when you first decided to bring a caregiver into your home. The most satisfying situation for you, your child(ren) and the caregiver is the one which most accurately reflects those values and circumstances you, as the parent, have previously defined. This will not be accomplished by an absentee parent.

When a Caregiver is Called "Mommy"

Young children are learning language. Many children use the term "Mommy" to describe adult women and "Daddy" for adult men. Mommy is also used to describe a woman who feeds, clothes, and cares for him. It is normal and desirable for your child to develop a loving attachment for his caregiver. This relationship can develop in addition to the strong bond you have with your child.

Strategies

If your child is calling his caregiver "mommy", here are a few strategies that you and your caregiver can use to help him learn the distinction between each person.

- Mount a picture of each of the significant people in his life on a separate index card and write their name under the photo. Cover the card with contact paper and attach the cards together with a ring.

- Request that the caregiver respond in the following way when the child calls her "mommy": "I'm your nanny and I love you very much. Your mommy is at work and she loves you very much too! Would you like to look at mommy's picture?"

- Both the parent and the caregiver can help the child make the transitions to the other's care by talking positively about the person soon to arrive. "I'm sure Vivian is on her way to our house now. Do you want to watch out the window for her?" "Mommy will be home soon, when we hear her car let's run to the door and give her a big hello."

Daily Routines: Consider the first thing you say to your child every morning. Greetings that include a big smile, special words (How is my favorite girl in the whole world today?), and gentle touch feel good to both parent and child. Repeated daily, this routine becomes an important part of your relationship. You can create a special connection during most any daily activity. As examples, you may give a piggy-back ride out of bed and to breakfast, treat them to a foot massage at bedtime, sing to stuffed animals while you and your child put them to bed at night, or give three kisses and three hugs at bedtime because they are three years old.

Connecting While You Are Gone: Many children enjoy talking with their parent at some time during the day. This works best for everyone when it is the same time every day. You can remind your child how much you love her in a note on the refrigerator or with a afternoon "surprise" snack you prepared for her each day. Older infants and toddlers will appreciate having a few pictures of the important people and animals in their lives laminated and put on a ring to keep them together.

Shared Activities: You can be a part of the day's activities. Create a story ("Once upon a time, there were three dogs who all liked to howl …") and have your child and caregiver add to it, or try making cookies with your son in the evening and have the two of them finish up during the day. Consider asking your caregiver to start some activities that you can finish with your child. A puzzle could be left for the two of you to complete

together, the child could draw half a picture and leave part for a parent to finish, or a card for grandma could be made and parent and child could finish up by decorating the envelope together.

Allow Time for Transitions: Upon returning home, slowly and gently enter the room and size up the activity. Some children may tell their parents to "go away," as they are busy having fun and are not ready to stop. If the caregiver is busy reading a book, sit and listen with your child. If they are playing a board game, you might sit and watch for a few minutes, and let them tell you when they are ready to move on. With so many things to do, it may be hard to just sit and be there, however, being there is just what your child needs to help make the transition from the caregiver to you.

Parent-Only Activities: Do not turn over all childcare activities to your caregiver. Retain some caregiving aspects for yourself. This might include preparing lunch for preschool, giving a bath, homework, bedtime rituals, and getting up in the night.

Have Fun: Don't let the tasks of the day keep you from spending time with your child where you are both physically and emotionally there for him. Get silly, be willing to put on dress-up clothes, dance around the house, and lie on the floor inside a homemade fort. Massage his feet at night, read his favorite book three times in a row, and pretend you are a puppy. These are the tasks of childhood—and staying connected involves sharing these important moments.

How to Spot Problems

How will you know if your caregiver is not providing the type of safe, nurturing, and stimulating care you intended them to give? Two important parts in evaluating the care your child(ren) is receiving are: first, being a visible, active partner in the care for your child(ren), and, second, knowing what to look for. At the beginning of a new caregiving relationship you will need to devote extra time to building a relationship with your caregiver, supporting your child(ren) in his adjustment to a new care situation, and checking in on the appropriateness of the caregiving environment.

In addition to developing effective communication strategies as described in Chapter 4, you will want to drop in on your caregiver and child(ren) unannounced. Your goal is to observe how the caregiver interacts with your child(ren) when she is in charge.

- As you enter your home, stop for a moment and listen. What do you hear? Laughter, singing, loud friendly monsters' voices, roaring lions, and the sounds of a story being told, or crying, fussing, whining, shouting, and loud violent sounds from the television.

- What do you see? Are there signs of busy, active play? Have new pictures been drawn, has a fort been built, are there trucks and animals all over the floor? These are all signs of a child who has been doing the important work of childhood, exploring, creating, and pretending.

- Are children being appropriately supervised? Are the bathroom doors kept closed to crawlers and toddlers? Are pot handles turned to the side or back of the stove? Are the foods she has offered them free of potential hazards such as choking? Has your infant been placed to sleep safely on her back, per your instructions, without pillows and blankets? Are toys with small pieces kept out of reach of children under three years of age?

- Is your caregiver engaged with your child(ren)? Does your caregiver make eye contact and talk quieting to your infant as she gives her the bottle or does she seem more interested in watching television than interaction? Is she talking to your son about his day while she changes his diaper or complaining about the messy diaper. Is your infant sitting on her lap turning the pages of a board book or sitting in an infant seat or swing alone? When you arrive, is she pushing your son on a swing, reading a story, dancing with the children around the room, sitting on the floor playing a board game? Or is she looking at a magazine or talking on the phone while the children are watching TV?

- If you happen to walk in on a child having a problem, how does caregiver respond? If a child has broken a rule does your caregiver explain the reason for the rule? Does she listen to children who are having a disagreement and help them problem solve a solution? Are negative emotions allowed as long as they are not hurtful to self, possessions, or others? Or are children who have problems (or are problems) automatically sent to their room for a time-out?

- How does your caregiver respond to your unannounced visit? Does she appear put out, resenting the intrusion into her day, or does she welcome and appreciate your involvement? Try to remember, children do not always have a good day and crying is not necessarily an indication of poor care. Your child could be screaming because he has been told that he can't have a cookie until lunch time. If you enter a situation like this, watch to see how your caregiver works with the child. Does she enforce the rule in a kind but firm manner? After a few minutes does the caregiver help the child move on by suggesting an alternative activity? "Michelle, how about if you and I read a story, or we could go outside and blow some bubbles."

- After listening, watching, and talking with your children and caregiver, you should review your feelings. Do you feel relieved because you found your child(ren) actively involved with a caregiver who is both loving and creative? Or does everything look good but for some reason you feel a pang in your gut? Is this because of your own conflicting feelings about leaving your child with someone else, or due to a tension you feel about the care your child(ren) is getting? Do not ignore your gut feelings. Address your concerns by spending more time with your caregiver. Try getting to know her as a person, inquiring about her day and continuing to drop in unexpectedly. If you are not using a daily log (as discussed in Chapter 4) with your caregiver, do so. Ask her to record the activities of the day as well as her observations about the high points and challenges of the day.

Video Surveillance

Some families include videotaping the interaction between caregiver and child(ren) as a strategy for spotting problems. In general, legal videotaping can only be done in public areas (not in the caregiver's bedroom or bathroom) *without* sound. Videotaping may be done either with the caregiver's knowledge or else secretly. Some employers include a release in their work agreement that gives them permission to tape without notifying the caregiver of the exact time of the taping. If done in secret, recording of sound violates federal wiretapping laws. Call the Attorney General's Office in your state to determine any local laws that pertain to this activity.

Should you consider video surveillance?

Pros:

- By notifying potential candidates that you plan to videotape, unqualified candidates may choose not to work for your family.
- You may find you have a wonderful caregiver.
- Upon viewing the tape, you may find problem areas due to miscommunication, which can be easily alleviated.
- You will be able to see a sample of the interactions that occur during the day. This may be particularly valuable with infants, who have difficulty articulating their feelings and concerns.
- Severe problems can be identified early, and the caregiver can be released from her duties.

Cons:

- Many caregivers feel that video surveillance is a violation of trust and respect, a necessary part of their working environment. Think how you would feel under the same circumstance.
- Families often substitute surveillance for other methods of monitoring the work environment, including dropping in unannounced and taking the time to develop a relationship with the caregiver.
- The video does not always provide a fair representation of the entire day or of a particular circumstance.

Some children adapt very easily to new situations and new people while others do not. Separation anxiety (crying and clinging to you when you are leaving) is common throughout the first six years of life. Separation problems in the beginning of a new child care arrangement should not be assumed to be a problem specific to this caregiver. You can work with your caregiver to develop a leaving routine. Give the older child some input into the routine. "How many kisses do you need, three or five, before I leave? I will honk the horn and flash the lights two times when I leave, does that sound good to you?" Never slip away without saying goodbye in hopes of avoiding a fuss, once the child realizes you are gone, he will become scared and his trust in you will be diminished. Even with a routine, some children will fuss when you leave. For most kids, the tears only last a few minutes and will taper off as they get use to the new schedule. Ask your caregiver to comfort the child during this period and then move on to help the child get involved in activity shortly after you leave.

What should you do if you suspect abuse? If you observe the caregiver abusing your child or the child has physical evidence of injuries, first provide for the immediate safety of your child and then call your local Child Protective Services or police. Each state has an agency required to receive and investigate reports of child abuse. You have a moral obligation to notify the authorities. If unreported, your caregiver is free to enter other employment where she may continue to harm children. Individuals who report in good faith are granted immunity from civil and criminal action.

Unfortunately, abuse is often not observed or obviously apparent. In this case you need to increase your daily contact with your caregiver. Institute a daily log where the caregiver is to record all injuries, accidents, and special concerns. Drop in on your caregiver during her work hours, recruit family members and friends to check in on your child(ren), and consider videotape surveillance. With increased communication you may find that your caregiver has observed the same behavior in your child and has concerns. If, however, you find your caregiver's explanation for injuries inconsistent with the injury or the caregiver is unresponsive or defensive in response to your concerns, consider calling Child Protective Services for advice. You only have to suspect your child is being mistreated to make that call. Calling your family doctor might also be a good idea.

Signs of Child Abuse

None of the symptoms below automatically signifies child abuse. Look for a clustering of clues, clues that are intense, that last more than a few days, come on suddenly, and are inappropriate for the child's age. For example, all children get bruises, however, bruises along with sadness and lack of a plausible explanation from the caregiver are signs for concern.

General Clues

- Behavior extremes (crying often or never, unusually aggressive, fearful, or withdrawn).
- Abusive to other children, animals, toys.
- Nervous, destructive, aggressive.
- Obsessive
- Appears sad.
- Fearful of adults.

Clues to Physical Abuse

- Bruises of various colors (indicating different ages).
- Injuries in the shape of an object (i.e., belt, rope, cord).
- Injuries inconsistent with information provided by caregiver.
- The child flinches when approached.

Clues to Emotional Abuse

- Withdrawn
- Apathetic
- Nervous tics.
- Lags in physical development.
- Lack of attachment to caregiver.

Clues to Sexual Abuse

- Difficulty sitting or walking.
- Inappropriate knowledge of sex.
- Evidence of trauma to mouth, genital, or anal areas.
- Reluctance to participate in physical activities.
- Poor peer relationships.
- Regressive behavior.

How you approach the dismissal of an in-home care provider will depend on the circumstances that prompt the action. The reasons for firing often fall under one of the following three categories:

- **Personality Conflicts:** The children like her well enough, she is reliable, but for some reason you have come to dislike her. It may not be anything that you can really pin down, you just don't like being around her or having her in your house.

- **Poor Job Performance:** She keeps a watchful eye on the children, but she doesn't seem to enjoy them. You've told her several times to make sure the children put their dirty clothes in the laundry hamper, get outside daily, and have an afternoon quiet time and yet none of these things being done.

- **Gross Negligence:** Lying, stealing, substance abuse, emotional instability, abusive behavior and bad judgment that endangers the children are all grounds for immediate firing.

In situations of gross negligence there is no question that firing is the appropriate course of action. When personality conflicts or minor job infractions exist the decision to keep or fire the caregiver may not be as easy. Families delay firing a caregiver for several reasons. These include:

- The time and energy it takes to hire a new caregiver.

- The disruption to your lives caused by having a gap in child care.

- The children like her.

- Concern about not being able to get a caregiver better then the current one.

- The agency guarantee has run out.

- The caregiver needs the job.

- You feel a sense of responsibility for having brought her to the country as an au pair.

At times, personality conflicts and poor job performance can be resolved by spending more time with the caregiver, getting to know her as a person, sitting down and clarifying your expectations, and improving daily communication. In the case of an au pair, local care coordinators from the placing agency are available for consultation on the difficulties you may be experiencing. Many nanny placement agencies also provide support to families and nannies in resolving differences.

It is time to make a change when the benefits no longer outweigh the limitations of the relationship. Using a caregiver should reduce the stress in your household. Your children should be active, happy, and thriving. They should be safe and you should feel at ease knowing that your caregiver is a positive presence in your household. When on balance these conditions do not exist, when difficulties cannot be readily resolved, it is time for a change.

You've decided to make a change, now you'll need to consider the following:

- **Timing:** If there is a best time to release a care provider it is at the end of her work day. If, however, you feel your children are not safe, act immediately! Tell your caregiver that you no longer need her services. Let her know when she can return to pick up her final check and any possessions she has at your home.

- **Review Your Agreement:** Before notifying the caregiver, you need to review your job agreement. Some contracts include a trial period in which either party can terminate the relationship without notice. Employees fired after this period customarily receive notice or severance pay.

- **Notice:** A period of one to three weeks' notice gives the employee an opportunity to look for a new position. It may be particularly difficult for a live-in employee to pick up and move without some notice.

- **Severance Pay:** is designed to help the caregiver cover her expenses while she is looking for a new job. Families usually give notice or severance pay but not both. Many families feel that once they've notified their caregiver of the need to make a change they want to sever ties immediately, and so choose to offer severance rather than notice.

- **Explaining the Problem:** What you tell your caregiver will depend on the relationship you have developed during the time she has been with you. If you have an open, honest relationship with the caregiver, she will likely appreciate hearing the truth. "I thought your gentle and quiet manner would have a calming effect on Tommy, but what I've come to believe is that he is a kid with a lot of energy and he needs a caregiver who is more like him." "Having someone who can be here every day by 7:00 A.M. is very important to me. I know it is hard for you to get here that early. I'm sorry we aren't able to make it work."

- **When to Be General:** If you think providing the specifics of the firing will anger your caregiver and possibly put your home or your family at risk, provide only general information. "I'm sorry, this care situation is not working out, I've decide to make a change."

- **References:** References are very important to caregivers. If your caregiver's performance was acceptable and your firing is the result of a personality conflict or mismatch between the caregiver and your child, offer to help your caregiver find a more suitable situation.

- **Safety Issues:** While your goal is for an amiable separation, that, unfortunately, is not always the case. An agitated caregiver might attempt to harm your home or your children. Safety precautions include changing your locks, your alarm code, your telephone calling card numbers and your school emergency cards. Notify your neighbors that this caregiver is no longer working for you and ask them to call you immediately if they see her near your home. Let your children know that they are not to talk to their former caregiver and definitely not go anywhere with her.

- **Paperwork:** If you are severing your relationship with your caregiver on the day of her firing, provide her with a brief letter of dismissal and a check to cover pay up to that date and any severance pay. Send a termination notice to the Unemployment Bureau and keep a copy of both the dismissal letter and termination notice in her employment file.

Telling the Children

Your explanation to your children will depend on their relationship with the caregiver and their ability to understand. A child who enjoys a good relationship with the caregiver will appreciate the opportunity to say goodbye. If the parting is amiable, and time allows, the strategies outlined earlier in Chapter 4 under Parting with a Loved One are appropriate (see page 74). When the situation necessitates the caregiver leaving without saying goodbye, help the child draw a goodbye picture or write a letter to the caregiver.

Change, even good change, results in stress. Do not overlook the impact of this change on your child. With the exception of infants, all children need to be told their caregiver will not be coming back. "Molly won't be coming to take care of you anymore. Grandma is going to stay with you until we find a new caregiver." You will minimize the impact of the change on your children if you maintain their daily schedules as much as possible, make extra time to spend with them and keep the chaos in your home to a minimum.

Checklist:

Lessons Learned

You should carefully examine your unsuccessful caregiving situation to help you find a better fit the next time around.

- Did your job description clearly reflect the job responsibilities?

- Does your situation require a person with more skill and experience than you previously anticipated?

- Do you pay enough to attract the right type of applicants?

- Did you take the time to interview several candidates?

- Was communication regular, open, and honest?

- Did you address concerns right away or did you avoid confrontations?

- Were you actively involved in making decisions about your child's daily care or did you allow the caregiver to dictate the care?

CHAPTER 6

Paperwork

The responsibilities of hiring a caregiver extend beyond the dynamics of your household. As an employer, you need also work within the strictures established by the government, which are designed to protect both you and your caregiver. The level of record-keeping and the legal requirements vary from state to state and by the type of child care you choose. According to the IRS, you are an employer if you pay someone to come into your home to care for your children. Employment tax is due on your care provider's wages if she earns $1,200 (at the time of this printing) in a calendar year. In some states, you must also pay state unemployment insurance tax. Babysitters under the age of 18 and enrolled in school are exempt from this requirement. Au pairs from bona fide programs are paid a living and education allowance and are also exempt from federal and state tax requirements. Depending on your state's policies, you may be required to pay or collect state employment taxes and provide worker's compensation insurance. Although all these additional responsibilities may seem intimidating at first glance, it is a simple matter to organize them if you follow the tips to the right. Your accountant can be very helpful with these matters, also.

Before you hire a caregiver, consider doing the following:

- Verify the applicant's right to work. The *Handbook for Employers* contains the regulations, procedures, and forms (I-9) required by the Immigration and Naturalization Service (INS). You can order a handbook or get additional information by calling the INS at 1-800-870-3676.

- Apply for an Employer Identification Number (EIN). You will need to include your EIN when reporting your household employment taxes. Form SS-4, Application for Employer Identification Number, describes both telephone and mail procedures for obtaining a number. It is available from certified public accountants and from IRS Forms and Publications at 1-800-829-3676.

- Get a copy of IRS's Publication 926, *Household Employer's Tax Guide*, explaining your federal tax requirements. It is a comprehensive guide to your federal obligations as an employer. It also contains a useful list of state unemployment tax agencies.

- Contact your state unemployment tax office to determine your state obligations as an employer. Remember to ask about policies regarding state income tax and unemployment insurance tax. You may be required to apply for a state employer identification number or numbers.

- Call your State Insurance Commissioner's office to determine if your state requires employers to purchase Workers' Compensation for domestic employees. Workers' Compensation (sometimes referred to as Disability Insurance) provides medical expenses and lost wages to employees who are injured on the job. It also protects the employer by covering the cost of defending lawsuits filed by injured employees. Some states provide coverage through a state-run fund and others required that it be purchased through a private carrier. Not all states require Workers' Compensation for domestic employees.

- Review your personal insurance policies with your agent. Even if you are not required by your state to purchase Workers' Compensation insurance, you may choice to do so by attaching a rider to your homeowner's/renter's policy. It is important that you have adequate coverage in case your care provider gets hurt on the job. If your caregiver will be driving your automobile, you will need to add her on your auto insurance policy.

Checklist

*You will need to withhold employ-
ment taxes if your care provider:*

- *Provides child care in your home
  and you set the standards for
  how the work is done.*

- *Receives wages based on salary
  or hours worked.*

- *Makes more than $1,200 in
  a year.*

- *Is over eighteen.*

- *Is not an au pair from a bona fide
  program.*

For any nonexempt caregivers employed during the year you must:

- Withhold and pay Social Security and Medicare taxes. The employer and the employee split the cost of these taxes, and the employer is required to withhold and remit the total amount.

- Pay federal unemployment insurance tax (FUTA). Refer to IRS Publication 926, *Household Employer's Tax Guide* for circumstances in which state unemployment insurance taxes impact the payment of federal unemployment taxes.

- Withhold federal income tax only if the employee requests it and if you agree. If you consent to withholding federal income tax, you will need to provide your caregiver with an Employee's Withholding Allowance Certificate (W-4) to complete. *Employer's Tax Guide*, Circular E, will help you determine the applicable rate of withholding for your caregiver. (Forms are available from certified public accountants and IRS forms and Publications at 1-800-829-3676.)

- Report all federal employment taxes you've withheld on your federal tax return by April 15th of each year. Consider that to avoid penalty you need to pay enough tax during the year to cover both the unemployment taxes associated with being an employer and your income taxes. As an employer, you have a couple of options, you can either (a) increase the withholding from your wages to cover the tax or (b) make estimated payments. Publication 919, *Is My Withholding Correct?* will help you estimate the correct amount of withholding and Form 1040-ES, *Estimated Tax for Individuals*, should be used to determine the appropriate amount of an estimated payment, if you choose that method of payment.

- Provide a yearly Wage and Tax Statement (W-2), to a caregiver for whom you paid Social Security and Medicare wages or for whom you withheld federal income tax. A copy of the W-2 is sent with Form W-3, Transmittal of Wage and Tax Statement, to the Social Security Administration.

- Meet all obligation, required by your state. (These may vary from state to state: in New York, for example, you must file quarterly.)

- Keep copies of all forms you file and records to substantiate the information you've provided. These include name, address, Social Security number, and wage and tax records.

Time sheets signed by employer and employee reduce the risk of misunderstandings and discrepancies. Your time sheet should list your caregiver's starting and ending time each day, total hours worked each day, overtime worked; and any sick, personal, or vacation time taken. Some families have their care provider complete the time sheet each pay period, while in other families both the care provider and parent keep a time sheet.

Don't forget that you are required by the Internal Revenue Service to keep detailed payroll records. It's important to be organized and consistent in your methods. There are several ways for you to meet this requirement. You can keep a detailed payroll log either by hand or with the aid of a computer payroll program, you can hire a payroll service or a bookkeeper, or you can utilize the services of an accountant. Several payroll services specific to "nanny taxes" can be accessed through the internet. If you use an accountant to handle your business and personal affairs, then it may be easy and prudent to have this person administer financial matters related to the caregiver, too. Information to be listed on your payroll record includes:

- Wages—gross and net
- Cash bonuses
- Extra compensation for additional hours.
- Reimbursements
- Any expense allowance paid.
- Vacation time
- Sick leave
- Personal leave
- Taxes withheld

Au Pair Requirements

According to au pair program regulations:

- Au pairs are to not to provide more than ten hours of child care on any given day and not more than 45 hours of child care per week.

- The au pair and the host family must sign a written agreement outlining the au pair's obligation to provide not more than forty-five hours of child care services per week.

- Au pairs are to receive a minimum of one-and-a-half days off per week in addition to one complete weekend off each month.

- Au pairs must register and attend classes offered by an accredited U.S. post secondary institution for not less than six semester hours [one year].

- Au pairs must receive two paid weeks of vacation per twelve-month time period.

Records to Keep

While meeting your state and federal obligations as an employer, you will amass a significant number of forms, publications, and documents, which support your actions. To prevent any future headaches, start early and keep accurate and complete files. Your care provider's basic information file should include the following:

- Full name, address, and phone number of employee.

- Copy of Social Security card

- Job application.

- Employment agreement.

- Dates of employment.

- Job performance evaluations.

- Form I-9 Verifying the Right to Work and copies of substantiating documents.

Consider keeping a second file designated to hold all payroll and tax information related to your caregiver. In this file you should keep:

- Time sheets.

- Detailed payroll records.

- A copy of your employee's W-4 (if you have agreed to withholding taxes).

- Record of date and amount of tax deposits made.

- Copies of state and federal tax returns.

- Records of fringe benefits provided.

- All federal and state employer ID numbers.

- Reference information such as state and federal employment and tax publications.

Useful IRS Publications and Forms

Household Employer's Tax Guide, Publication 926

Application for Employer Identification Number, Form SS-4

Employee's Withholding Allowance Certificate, Form W-4

Transmittal of Wage and Tax Statements, Form W-3

Employer's Tax Guide, Publication 15, Circular E

Is My Withholding Correct? Publication 919

Estimated Tax for Individuals, Form 1040-ES

Household Employment Taxes, Schedule H

Child and Dependent Care Expenses, Publication 503

To order IRS publications and forms call 1-800-829-3676.

Time sheets signed by employer and employee reduce the risk of misunderstandings and discrepancies. Your time sheet should list your caregiver's starting and ending time each day, total hours worked each day, overtime worked; and any sick, personal, or vacation time taken. Some families have their care provider complete the time sheet each pay period, while in other families both the care provider and parent keep a time sheet.

Time Sheet

Pay period beginning: ___/___/___ and ending ___/___/___

Date	Start Time	End Time	Total Hours	Overtime

Total hours worked: _____

Total hours overtime: _____

Sick leave, personal leave, or vacation taken: _____

Employee signature: _____ Date: _____

Employer signature: _____ Date: _____

Two different strategies allow parents a tax break for child care expenses. These are the dependent care account (DCA) and the tax credit for child or dependent care.

Dependent Care Account (DCA): Check to see if your employer offers dependent care accounts as a benefit. If so, you can contribute several thousand pretax dollars of your annual salary to this account. Depending on the IRS requirements for any particular year, money from this account can then be used to cover child care expenses.

Tax Credit for Childcare: If you don't have access to a DCA, you may qualify for the tax credit for child or dependent care on your federal income taxes. Families who qualify can take a percentage of their child care costs at this printing, up to $2,400 for one child or $4,800 for two or more. Refer to IRS Publication 503, *Child and Dependent Care Expenses* to see if you are eligible for this tax credit.

Our Story

One Family's Paper-Management Strategies

"It helps to be organized from the beginning. We keep a file on our nanny that includes basic information like name, address, Social Security number, and emergency contacts. For payroll and taxes we use a bookkeeping program on our computer. It's great! It keeps track of wages, taxes, vacation, and sick leave and prepares all the tax forms we need."

Determining Your Costs

While wages will be your largest outlay, several other costs are associated with in-home child care. Since expenses can vary greatly from one region to another, this worksheet is designed to help you assess costs and compare them. Make a few copies and then fill out the sheet to weigh expenses for each of the options you are considering.

CHECK IF INCURRING THIS EXPENSE	EXPENSE CATEGORIES	ESTIMATED COST (ONE TIME OR MONTHLY)

Hiring Expenses

_____ Placement fee _____

_____ Advertisements _____

Wages

_____ Salary or hourly _____

_____ Overtime _____

_____ Vacation Pay _____

_____ Paid Holidays _____

_____ Sick Time _____

_____ Personal Leave _____

Taxes

_____ Social Security and Medicare _____

_____ Federal Unemployment Insurance _____

_____ State Unemployment Insurance (if required) _____

Benefits

_____ Workers' Compensation Insurance (not required in all states, highly recommended even if not required) _____

_____ Health Insurance _____

_____ Room and Board _____

_____ Telephone _____

_____ Club Memberships _____

_____ Gas Allowance or Mileage Allowance _____

_____ Educational Benefit _____

_____ Bonuses and Gifts _____

Record Keeping Costs

_____ Accountant _____

_____ Domestic Employer Tax Service _____

_____ Record Keeping Program for Computer _____

Other

_____ Increased utilities from having child and caregiver in home all day _____

_____ Cost of equipping home for a live-in nanny or au pair _____

_____ Upkeep on car provided for caregiver _____

_____ Back up child care (to cover when caregiver is on vacation, or taking sick leave) _____

Personalized Caregiver's Book

Step into your caregiver's shoes for a minute. You have just accepted a new job caring for a family's most special members, their children. No matter how much training and experience you have, it will take time to get to know this family. Not only will you will need to learn about each child's personality, daily schedule, favorite foods, rituals, and best friends, you will also need to find out the rules unique to this home (i.e., no shoes worn inside, no cookies before lunch), where the water cut-off valve is in case of an emergency, and how to work the security system. A lot of important information is given during the first few days. Will your caregiver be able to remember it all?

You can help your caregiver feel confident and welcome by preparing a notebook especially for her. The following pages have been designed to help you create such a book. Copy each of the following pages and place in a three-ringed notebook. Organize the book for easy access with tabs labeled Basic Information, Children, Safety, and Home/Car. Provide blank pages for her to make notes and compose questions. If you want, personalize your book by adding a picture of your family, children's drawings, or by having your children decorate the outside with stickers. If you have an infant, you might want to write a letter to the caregiver from the infant, telling her what cues your baby uses to communicate when she's hungry, tired, or just needs to be cuddled. Be sure to include information about any special medical conditions or other features your caregiver will need to know about your family, home, or neighborhood. A caregiver new to the area will definitely appreciate a map and a list of places to see and shop.

In addition to being greatly appreciated by your caregiver, this book will help you clarify your expectations, establish a system for daily communication and organize all your important information in one convenient location.

The following

Welcome to Our Family

section was designed for you to copy

and give to your new care provider

as a handy guide to your family.

Welcome to Our Family

a write-in handbook just for you

From: The _____ family

To: _____

Welcome to the _____ family.

We are looking forward to getting to know you and we prepared this booklet to help you get to know us.

[place picture here]

The adults in our family include: _____ , who is _____
and _____ , who is _____
and _____ , who is _____

The children in our family are:

_____ who is _____ years old and whose favorite things are
_____

_____ who is _____ years old and whose favorite things are
_____

_____ who is _____ years old and whose favorite things are
_____

Some important things about our family include:

_____
_____
_____
_____

Important Information You Need to Know:

We live at _____ and the nearest cross street is _____
Our phone number is _____

Parents' Numbers

Dad's daytime number _____ Cell phone _____
pager _____
Mom's daytime number _____ Cell phone _____
pager _____

EMERGENCY NUMBERS:

Medical emergency _____ Poison control _____
Police department _____ Fire dept _____

Health Care Information

Children's doctor _____ Phone number _____
Address _____
Insurance policy number _____

Hospital of choice _____ Phone number _____
Address _____
Special medical notes _____
_____
_____

First aid supplies are located _____
Children's dentist _____ Phone number _____
Address _____
Insurance policy number _____
Veterinarian _____ Phone number _____
Address _____

Our Special Family, Friends, Neighbors, Teachers

_____ Phone _____ She/he is _____
(relationship)
_____ Phone _____ She/he is _____
(relationship)
_____ Phone _____ She/he is _____
(relationship)
_____ Phone _____ She/he is _____
(relationship)

In Case of a
Medical Emergency or Accident

Unfortunately, accidents happen and not always when children are at home. We have made two copies of this form, one for this book and the other to go with you and the children on outings.

If one of the children is hurt please follow these steps;

1. Determine if it is life threatening. If yes, call 911 immediately.

2. For bumps, scrapes, and minor ouchies, please administer the appropriate first aid and lots of love. Be sure and list all minor incidents in your daily log, so we will be able to continue the course of treatment.

3. If it is not life threatening, but more than a minor hurt, call a parent immediately.

Dad's daytime number _____

Cell phone _____

Mom's daytime number _____

Cell phone _____

3. If a parent is not available, call the child's doctor.

Children's doctor _____ Phone number _____

Address _____

Insurance policy _____

Meals and Snacks

When _____
_____
_____

What is to be served _____
_____
_____
_____

Favorite foods _____
_____
_____
_____

Foods not to be served _____
(Including foods that are a choking hazard for children under four.)
_____
_____
_____

Where food can be eaten _____
_____
_____
_____

Manners to observe _____
_____
_____
_____

Meal clean up _____
_____
_____
_____

Dressing and Resting

When _____

What _____

_____

Laundry procedures _____

_____

Bathing/cleanliness _____
Bathing _____

Teeth brushing _____

_____

Hair care _____

Resting times _____
Nap times _____

Nap rituals _____

_____

Activities

Scheduled activities _____

_____

_____

Children's indoor play areas _____

_____

_____

How play areas are to be maintained _____

_____

_____

Outside activities and play areas _____

_____

_____

_____

_____

Some ideas for stimulating growth and development

_____

_____

_____

_____

Outings

Favorites are _____

_____

_____

_____

_____

Getting together with other children

Friends are _____

_____

_____

_____

_____

_____

_____

_____

_____

_____

How We Spent Our Time Together

Our Daily Log

Child's name _____

Date _____

Parent comments _____

_____

_____

_____

_____

_____

_____

_____

_____

_____

Meals and Snacks

Time _____

What I ate and how much _____

_____

_____

_____

_____

_____

_____

_____

Elimination

Time _____

Comments _____

_____

_____

_____

_____

_____

_____

Naps

Time _____

Length _____

Comments _____

_____

_____

_____

_____

_____

_____

_____

Activities

_____

_____

_____

_____

_____

_____

_____

_____

Bumps, Scrapes, and Ouchies

Challenges

Successes

The Tough Times

You are an important person in helping our child(ren) learn appropriate behaviors. It is normal for children to display challenging behavior; to make mistakes because they the lack the experience, skills, and self-control of adults; and to test the rules to make sure that you really mean what you say. One way to deal with tough situations is to think ahead and prevent difficult situations from happening in the first place.

Our most effective prevention strategies are:

_____

_____

_____

_____

_____

_____

The rules and consequences we have in our family are:

_____

_____

_____

Common problems and strategies are:

_____

_____

_____

_____

_____

_____

_____

Things to do if the child(ren) are driving you crazy
(we all have those days):

_____

_____

_____

_____

_____

Discipline that is not acceptable includes:

_____

_____

_____

_____

_____

_____

Keeping Safe

Our family has established the following safety rules and procedures:

Inside Our Home

General rules _____

_____

_____

In the kitchen _____

_____

_____

In the bathroom _____

_____

_____

_____

In the bedroom _____

_____

_____

Outdoor play areas _____

_____

_____

_____

Street _____

_____

_____

Sun protection _____

_____

_____

When on Outings

Staying together _____

If separated _____

In the Car

Where children may sit _____

_____

_____

How children are to be restrained _____

_____

_____

Safety rules to be observed by the driver _____

_____

_____

_____

If we all follow these precautions, we will reduce the likelihood of injury. The single most important thing that you can do to insure our child(ren)'s safety is to provide appropriate supervision.

Using the Car

The car may be used for: _____

_____

_____

_____

_____

The car may not be used in the following situations:

_____

_____

_____

_____

How the car is to be fueled _____

_____

_____

Our expectations of cleanliness _____

_____

_____

_____

Regular maintenance _____

_____

_____

_____

Spare keys: _____

Alarm system: _____

Stereo system: _____

Car phone: _____

Be sure and notify us if an indicator light comes on or if the car begins to respond strangely.

In case of any accident

The auto registration and insurance are located

_____

Never leave the scene of an accident.

Call the police immediately.

Call us.

House Rules

Every family has rules regarding the care and use of their home. Sometimes these rules are unspoken. We have tried to list all our rules here in order to prevent possible misunderstandings.

_____

_____

_____

_____

Some special things about our home include:

_____

_____

_____

Spare keys: _____

_____

Alarm system: _____

_____

Keeping track of supplies: _____

_____

Refrigerator: _____

_____

Dishes: _____

_____

Pet rules: _____

_____

_____

Telephone Procedures

How we would like you to answer the phone

_____

_____

How messages are to be taken

_____

_____

How to retrieve messages

_____

_____

How to record messages

_____

_____

Rules regarding your personal use of the telephone

_____

_____

Our rules about drugs and alcohol are:

_____

_____

Our rules about visitors are:

_____

_____

_____

Just in Case Something Goes Wrong

Places to Find the Following

Fuse box _____

Fire extinguishers _____

Fire exits _____

Smoke detectors _____

Flashlights _____

Emergency/earthquake safety spot _____

Water cut-off valve _____

Other Important Information

Security phone number _____

Alarm instructions and code _____

Alarm company phone number _____

Water company _____

Cable company _____

Power company _____

Phone company _____

To Kim for years of loving care.

Acknowledgments

My heartfelt thanks to:
Boz Kalange, Deborah Ferguson, Carol Dugdeon, Debbie McGee,
Diane Lemonides, Joe DeNicholas, Sandy Weibort, Margaret Ball,
Anne-Luise Janssen, Jennifer Mearns, and Anna Nilsson
for sharing their experiences and wisdom
on what makes a successful child care situation.

Nancy Halter, of EF Au Pair for her willingness to provide information
on the au pair program, and locate families for my interviews.

Rebekah Zincavage at the Boston Nanny Center
for guiding me to families with experience and a willingness to share.

Mary Clurman, of Apple Pie USA Nannies and Nanny News
for back issues, and her invaluable and timely response to my queries.

About the Author

Jerri Wolfe is a certified family life educator with an M.S. in education and a Ph.D. in family resource management. The last fifteen years she has served in a variety of parent education capacities. These include, developing curriculum for hospital based parent education programs, providing training and technical support for parent educators, programs administrators and policy makers and most importantly working directly with parents throughout the Pacific Northwest. Dr. Wolfe is trained as a parent-child interaction specialist and has served as a Child Development Specialist for Bellevue Community College in Washington State. During her eleven years in the Seattle area she lectured to community organizations and Fortune 500 companies about strategies for meeting the challenges of combining employment and family life. A resident of Corvallis, Oregon, she serves as a parent educator for the Healthy Start Program of Linn County.

About the Illustrator

Sally Lee is an illustrator and painter who lives in Danvers, Massachusetts. She is frequently published in *Worldlink* and *IEEE* magazines, and recently collaborated with Jean Lee on the children's book, *Today I Sat*. Sallyolee@aol.com

INDEX